CATHOLIC ACTION

by ABBÉ G. MICHONNEAU

Translated by
EDMOND BONIN

AND THE PARISH

AND ABBÉ R. MEURICE

THE NEWMAN PRESS

Westminster, Maryland

1955

This is a translation of
Pour une action paroissiale efficace,
Number 43 in the series *"Rencontres"*
published by Les Editions du Cerf, Paris

Nihil obstat: Edward A. Cerny, S.S.,D.D.
Censor Librorum
Imprimatur: Francis P. Keough, D.D.
Archbishop of Baltimore
July 11, 1955

All quotations from the New Testament are taken from the Confra-
ternity of Christian Doctrine edition, 1947; quotations from the Old
Testament are from the Douay version.

Library of Congress Catalog Card Number: 55–8652
Copyright, 1955, by THE NEWMAN PRESS
Printed in the United States of America

CONTENTS

PART ONE

RELIGIOUS MAKE BETTER

SHEPHERDS

by

ABBÉ G. MICHONNEAU

CHAPTER I

THE MEANING OF "PARISH"
AND "VOCATION"

The word "parish" covers everything from towns in
Brittany or eastern France to some section of a province,
a zone of Paris or a suburban community

Can the priests in such different localities have the
same outlook? Will a pastor in Vendée have the same
views, plans, worries and projects as one in Argenteuil
or Kremlin-Bicêtre? Canon Law imposes the same rules
on both men. Still, can people and things look the same
to the village priest who knows there is a family of practicing Catholics behind every door and the city priest
who is not too sure what door to knock on? Is it possible
that these two men, whose work is designated by the
same term though it is so dissimilar and is performed
under diametrically opposed conditions, are of the same
mold? Both of them are pastors and the two spheres entrusted to them are currently described by the one word
"parish."

In country districts, "parish" is easy to define. Its
limits are those of the community; it is territorial as well

as personal. Look at the map: where one parish ends, another begins. There is no question of continuity. When, on the contrary, a suburbanite speaks of "my parish" or "the parish" in general, you have to listen for a moment to see whether he means those who practice the faith or those who happen to live within the parish limits.

In this connection, does the expression "a de-Christianized parish" make sense? If it refers to an area where the people, though baptized and possessing the faith, no longer live according to the gospel or fulfill their religious duties, the expression is correct since it denotes a parish which was Christian once but is no longer so. But if the term is applied to a place where a fervent community of believers dwells in the midst of a larger group who, for the most part, have never had the faith, then it is difficult to see who or what can be labeled "de-Christianized." Could it be the faithful? No, because they are fervent—perhaps more fervent than they would be in a Christian country, where social pressure often forces one to go to church. Could it be the non-believers, those who do not frequent the sacraments? Hardly, since they have never been Christians at all.

Shall we, then, have to give a precise meaning to the word "parish" as used in this book? To be logical, we should choose one definition and stick to it; but that is exactly what we do not want to do. Always mindful of suburban parishes, we would rather not restrict the term "parish" to the Christian community any more than we would want to equate it simply with the confines of a parish.

We are glad that the word designates both believers and the multitude of half-believers or total unbelievers. We are glad that it focuses our attention and thought on those who "come to church" as well as on those who do not, for the simple reason that we do not want to abandon one group or forget the other.

We do not wish to choose, because choosing means sacrificing something and the true shepherd of souls cannot consent to that. We are glad that the word "parish" reminds us of all our pastoral duties at once and that the very mention of it conjures up both the joy and the anguish of a shepherd of souls.

The word "parish" is dear to us because it is synonymous with being drawn and quartered. When I say "my parish," the "my" is not a possessive pronoun; much like a personal pronoun, rather, it expresses the utter gift of myself—all that I am and have—which I must make to the parish entrusted to me. As for this task to which I must devote myself, I want it to serve two ends: to help faithful souls draw near to God, and silently to call all who do not and cannot know of Him, those I constantly desire to reach.

The Code of Canon Law has often been criticized for legislating for dechristianized countries as if they were still Christian, and we in the ministry have frequently deplored the lack of a spiritual code to follow in mission territory. Yet is that not proof of great feeling on the part of the Church, who refuses to brand definitively as infidel the vast domains of early Christendom? She cannot bring herself to call "pagan" those countries where the material cross of Christ still stands and which not only belonged to the Church but *were* the Church for so many centuries.

The Church is both the far-flung lands where missionaries go and the faith-fed lands whence missionaries come. The Church is the community of Christians whose divine and human dynamism leavens the whole dough of mankind; and because of that, the parish—which is essentially a part of the Church, which is the Church in a given territory—can no more choose between believers and unbelievers than we can choose between yeast and dough and forsake one to concentrate on the other.

We regret having to spend so much time splitting hairs but it so happens that, from the very beginning of our little book on the pastoral and religious vocation, the word "parish" assumes the power of a symbol and a standard. In its several connotations it summarizes our whole call: a call to be shepherds and missioners, a call to arouse and bring the community together, a call to be ready for any task and accessible to everyone.

"My parish"—the expression makes me think immediately of the huge crowds entrusted to my care, whom I do not know, and, doubtlessly, shall never know because it would be humanly impossible to do so. But I want the words to summon up each and every soul I have charge of, regardless of class or social standing,

regardless even of beliefs; and at the same time I want
to say they are "mine"—even those who hate me, and
those on the furthest fringe of the parish morally or
territorially.

When I say "my parish," I want to remember that
group of the faithful—small as it may be—which surrounds me with its faith, prayer and activity. I want to
recall every adolescent and adult, every home, every
sodality. I want to evoke the atmosphere of Sunday
Mass and each tiny community in the neighborhood
which is striving to live the gospel throughout the week.
I want to include those who knock at my door and sit
waiting for a word of cheer. It is not enough for me to
remember that community, whether large or small, afire
or just kindling. No, I must understand that it is the
scene of my labors; it is where I can work like yeast in
dough; it is the life cell I have to nourish since it is in
and through that community that the greater part of
the work must be done. What I count on is that group
and the numberless ways it can amplify and supplement
my work as keeper of souls. Only in and because of it—
since it is the Church and therefore the body of Christ
—can I look at the vast field around me without being
crushed by the job to be done.

"My parish" means the best I can discover among the
treasures Christ has given me to distribute, all I can
give, and all the inspiration I can find living among
those who understand; but it also includes the ceaseless
sorrow I feel for those who do not know and do not

want to know. Giving life to my parish means living Christ, living His life, His teaching, His apostolic love.

"My parish" sums up all my sufferings and joys, my cares and my hopes. It expresses all I willed when, as a young man, I glimpsed the priestly calling: celebrating the mysteries, preaching the word, and spreading the kingdom of God.

That is why any attempt to limit the sense of "parish" would rob it of its missionary implications, and, by that very fact, of all that makes it meaningful to us. It would be killing the word, the way you kill a living thing by mutilating it or depriving it of those stimuli it needs for growth.

We have refused to restrict the meaning of "parish," then, for fear of narrowing our outlook. Let us now try to see what this outlook, this perspective, is.

Occasionally we find a boy who likes to re-enact church ceremonies at home, makes himself an altar, candelabra and vestments, and officiates at the services. People predict he will become a priest, and when questioned he avers, "Yes, I will say Mass some day."

Can any of that mean he has a real calling? Is it a sign of a vocation? An expert at recruiting seminarians once replied, "Surely. It's a sign he's called to be a sacristan."

Nevertheless, many vocations have come to light during this sort of play-acting. The young celebrant, now

an altar boy, has become familiar with the real ceremonies; he loves the ritual, public prayer and all the
feasts. The thought of consecrating his life to this
warms his heart and he enters the seminary, where the
call and his response to it grow deeper as he gains a
broader understanding of the life and labors that lie
ahead of him as a priest. Thus does an altar boy's
dream develop into a genuine missionary vocation.

It would be unfortunate if a priest, especially a pastor,
saw merely the liturgical aspect of his duties; for, after
all, parish life means more than worship or the administering of the sacraments. We agree that the Mass,
especially Sunday Mass, is the precious leaven that lets
a parish rise and take shape and grow strong. We agree,
too, that the parish is the real "home" of the sacraments,
that one of its most urgent tasks is to teach the people
how great and vitally necessary each sacrament is, and
that pastors and assistants are at the disposition of any-
body who asks to receive one. Never can we priests prize
these channels of grace at their true value or administer
them with too much love. I pity the priest who is not
happy in his church. I pity the pastor or the curate who
does not feel at home with his congregation; who fails
to experience the deep joy of the Lord's Day spent
among the praying and singing throng; who cares little
to officiate at ceremonies, conscious of being responsible
for the fervor of all; and who cannot taste the tremendous thrill of giving Communion. No priest can forget the long hours spent in the confessional. The priest

must be happy in everything related to the sacraments, and, indeed, "everything related to the sacraments" is an extremely important part of his work in the parish.

Still, it is only a part and not the whole story. His activity, his mission, is not limited to that. The parish is the agent that awakens, animates, guards, broadens and deepens Christianity in a given territory, in relation to which territory the parish is a part of the Church and has almost as broad a mission as the Church.

Some seem to think that, in a parish, the Church's mission is restricted to the liturgical life. We would be seriously tempted to say with Bishop Blanchet, "A parish that has only been 'preserved' is one that has yet to be won over." At any rate, the Church's mission is far broader and more complex in areas which are predominantly unbelieving.

For the parish—which is part of the Church on the march—does that mean simply some sort of adaptation, more or less difficult according to locality, more or less successful according to the capability of the clergy? Can a parish be said to have the missionary spirit merely because it is the scene of a few minor revolutions or of ceremonies so designed as to be accessible to the masses and especially the common people?

We may say Mass facing the congregation, with explanations and hymns in the vernacular. We may reorganize sodalities and make them appealing to the young. By looking around and evaluating them we may discover and successfully use methods and formulas which have proved efficacious elsewhere. Our parish will then be a combination of societies which will periodically renew their source of appeal but always continue to group together, under the guidance of the parish clergy (as completely and actively as the clergy's intelligence and zeal warrant), the few souls who want to feed on the choice food set aside for them, and, in return, agree to remain faithful.

Yet, can that group be called a parish, a living parish, a missionary parish, or, more exactly, a part of the Church? A parish is that portion of humanity which lives within the area assigned to a pastor; and his responsibility, his essential mission, is to insure that this portion of humanity sees a genuine witnessing to the gospel in its midst. His work is not over when he has tended to parish business or taken care of the faithful. His work is something more than that: something indefinite—not only what he gives, what he is or does; but a spoken or unspoken sermon, the very life, activity and demeanor of the parish he quickens. His work is not done until that witness, like the yeast which imparts its strength to the lump of dough, is brought to the most destitute and errant, the most indifferent and hostile of men.

Understanding the vocation of the parish and of the parish priest means understanding the urgency and the scope of their work; understanding it not as a utilitarian need of our times but as the very power of Christ for the salvation of the world; understanding that it is the deep-down growth and the vital force of that mustard seed sown on earth two thousand years ago; understanding that that seed is none other than the word of God which has called us and still calls all Christians and ceaselessly troubles "every man who comes into this world."

But the question is precisely this: Can parish work still bear witness to the gospel? Can the parish be a field where the seed of Christ may grow? After seeing the near-lethargy of certain parishes and the amorphous groups of worshipers in some churches, we can well ask whether parishes have not become bloodless bodies or sapless branches no longer capable of receiving life. It is an undeniable fact that the sight of such paralyzed parishes presents a serious problem to the young man who wants to work in the vast fields the Master says are ripe for the harvest. He has reason to ask himself with great concern, "Is that where, having dedicated myself unreservedly, I can best answer Christ's call and do really effectual work for Him?"

We shall try to answer that question in the next chapter. Before doing so we must say this: If, in judging the effectiveness of parish work, we consider only lifeless parishes, we already know the answer. But it would be almost as surely discouraging to judge from the failures or seeming ineffectiveness of certain parishes which have done everything they could to produce results. They made, or thought they were making, all necessary adjustments, nor did they hesitate to use any means that seemed good. They even gave a new life to the community. But they did not give it its full share of power or let it grow to its proper dimensions. They used methods and systems and imposed them in such a way as to wear them threadbare and make them forever useless for anyone else.

The explanation lies in a lack of synthesis, of something to serve as a keystone to the whole edifice—which keystone may very well have been that final wholehearted welcoming of the common man, that final thoroughgoing spirit of daring and enterprise.[1] Because

---

[1] We should like to give a few examples of ineffective changes.

As regards the liturgy: To give life to the various services, some churces read and comment on the text used; but not everyone in the congregation has the same text. Other churches provide missals for the faithful but do not consider whether the translation is adapted to their intellectual level, intelligible and interesting; or they simply give them books to use as best they can. Still others read and comment, but in such a hieratic fashion as to remedy the situation not a bit. And in many parishes it is the curate, or the pastor alone, who is trying to effect the minor revolution. Such cases betray ignorance of the problem. What is needed is a profound transformation—changing a drowsy congregation into a fervent community. There is so much laziness to be overcome that the change cannot be wrought by external means or without the united effort of the various militant groups within the parish.

As regards the money question: With the best intentions in the world, a pastor may abolish budget envelopes but expound the problem of money to individuals and families so insistently that they feel obliged to give more than they reasonably should. Another no longer exacts a fee for the first Holy Communion ceremony, but on his desk he places a box in which the parents

there was no synthesis there was no seed; because there was no keystone there was no edifice. But that does not prove that the seed cannot exist and mature elsewhere or that the building cannot be built in some other place.

---

may place a "voluntary" offering. A third one has gone further and does not even use the box; yet the greater part of his Sunday sermon is devoted to studying the parish's financial situation. In any case, the results—apostolically speaking—are negligible.

We could mention other matters—accessibility, the apostolate, Catholic Action—and give examples of half measures. Even though the work to be done in one sphere has been clearly comprehended and accomplished, the fact that nothing has been done in some other sphere is enough to render the best intentions fruitless. Our trouble, it seems, is that we do not see, feel or think for ourselves. We are afraid to act.

CHAPTER II

CURES, NOT SINECURES

The greatest danger a parish priest runs is that of being locked within a little circle of practicing Catholics, trapped by his very priestly activity on behalf of a group of the faithful who monopolize his time, his person, his labors and may lead him to think that the life of the whole world is conditioned by and modeled on the life of this tiny cell.

Such groups have been called artificial, but they are not. If they were, they would be harmless because artificiality is soon routed by the exigencies of life and practical living. The truth is that these milieux are restricted. But society is full of little groups which draw a magic circle around themselves and avoid others as sedulously as others avoid them. Like all such cliques, these pious ones live after the manner of microcosms; and that is exactly what is wrong with them, for their isolation is diametrically opposed to the gospel ideal which should animate them. As we have said, a truly Christian community exists—and exists in a particular manner—solely because it is the yeast in the dough and must lose its life to find it anew with the masses. Usually, however, the coteries in a parish shut themselves off, become self-sufficient, and devote all their attention and activity to their own interior perfection.

It is easy to see how this spirit and its sclerotic effects might frighten a seminarian as he reflects on parish work and wonders whether he too will have to narrow his life and his dreams down to such dimensions and time them once for all to such a sleepy rhythm. On entering the seminary, a young man keeps vivid recollections of what he saw in the world. Only yesterday he was living like all his friends, sharing the same work and studies and pastimes. He grew up among country people, factory workers or students; and if called to the priesthood relatively late, he may have been an engineer or a doctor, a merchant or a mechanic. There is a sudden, drastic change between his life in the world and his life in the seminary.

Now, he has answered the call to the priesthood precisely because he wants to evangelize that part of humanity whence he comes. Having sensed its moral and spiritual wretchedness and measured the dreadful distance separating his old companions from the Church and Christ, he has willed to consecrate his entire life to bringing the Church and Christ back to them. The sight of the deep moat that estranges the modern world, and especially the working class, from Christ, and the desire to work with all his might to bridge it—these two things constituted for him his missionary vocation.

Is it surprising, then, that when contemplating parish work he is afraid—afraid of being snapped up and imprisoned or at the very least cramped by the environment in which he would enter? He goes to the seminary, not to forget the place he comes from, but rather to think of it all the more, to think of it all through life. He has dreamed of being a contact man between that milieu and the Church, and now he is afraid of becoming a sort of high priest isolated in the sanctuary.[1]

This fear seizes not only the candidate who enters the seminary late in life. Unless quite chloroformed by their mode of living, so many of those who have spent years in juniorates and minor seminaries look with wide-open eyes upon the world around them and are overwhelmed by that same dread: "What shall we do if our whole life is to be spent on the parish treadmill?" How many major seminarians and young priests are alarmed at such a prospect!

A few decades ago, earnest seminarians would spend several weeks of their vacation helping the pastor conduct summer schools or camps. They became very enthusiastic over this type of work—and, fortunately, many still do. Knowing nothing else, they conceived their whole future ministry in terms of groups and teams to be organized. Every one of them had worked out his

[1] In the original French this sentence contains an untranslatable play on words: "He has dreamed of being a bridge (*pont*) between that milieu and the Church, and now he is afraid of becoming a *pont*iff isolated in the sanctuary." (Translator's note.)

own theory—a very definite one, too—and seminary walks were loud with tireless discussions on this method and that.

Until forbidden to do so by Rome, seminarians used to take advantage of vacation time to acquire experience in agriculture, industry, commercial fishing, newspaper hawking and many other fields where they discovered immense throngs who had yet to be evangelized since they were quite outside the parish's scope of influence.

For it is a fact that present-day living has divided life itself into zones which are by no means territorial. Some sections of the working class resemble the company which was building a dam in the mountain village where I remember going to say Mass one Sunday. Chatting with the parishioners after Mass, I asked how many practicing Catholics there were in the parish.

They answered, "Everybody here goes to Mass, and the pastor keeps in touch with all of us."

"And is he welcome when he visits the company sheds?"

"Oh," they blurted in amazement at my question, "he doesn't go there. Those people never come to church, and Father doesn't go to see them. They're not part of the parish."

There is an example of a parish ignoring a group of laborers. And what about parishes that stand in their midst and yet drive them away? A huge mill opens in some town and draws all hands from the surrounding

countryside. The management builds them a little world
of uniform houses and creates everything in it—co-op-
eratives, social centers, and even a church. It goes further and places a "pastor" at the entire disposition of
the workers. This looks like a magnificent piece of work,
and it may be; but it may also make the worker look
upon the "parish" as a creation of the management and
consequently as something which is not for him.

Hospitals, especially sanatoriums, training centers and
agricultural schools wall off life into definite compart-
ments. There are even vaster sectors of thought which
eventually become sectors of life, little worlds all by
themselves: the world of the movies, the theater, and
others as remote as they are inaccessible to us. When
discussing work and leisure with a casual acquaintance,
we have often been astonished to find him living with
others in a completely engrossing—and, to us, quite
unknown—world of occupations and thoughts and feel-
ings and interests.

Now, all these sectors, because they constitute very
special milieux, are totally and almost necessarily beyond
the influence of any parish. It is becoming clearer and
clearer that plans for apostolic and social action must
transcend the hierarchical mapping out of the Church.
We must think and act in terms of cities, geographical
regions and nations. The fact that there are several
parishes in a country town may facilitate assistance at
church services, but does it facilitate activity on a wide
scale? At every step specialized Catholic Action comes

up against parish boundaries. The workingman's world knows no such boundaries and middle-class families pay even less attention to them in their social dealings. Neither can civic and municipal business take account of them. If Catholics, then, want to campaign for proper housing, peace, or anything else, why should their efforts be restricted to the boundaries or the active members of one parish rather than another? Should not the whole town work together? In some sections any apostolic labor has to be organized from the regional viewpoint. With regard to a country as a whole, obviously such work can hardly be fitted into the artificial molds of dioceses. By the very fact that specialized Catholic Action must adapt itself to the various phases of life which it seeks to affect, it has highlighted these problems and made us realize that we must solve them.

As everyone admits, specialized Catholic Action is essential to the development of Christianity today. We may even say it is the authentic form of that development. This is nothing new. There has long been a universe of private worlds—for instance, the world of commercial fishermen—which have nothing to do with territorial limits. Still, in the past, that did not keep such men, drudges though they were, from thinking of themselves as belonging to a parish, basing their Christian life on it and gladly returning to it to fulfill their duties as good parishoners. Father Lowe reminds us that the dockers he met in Marseille seem to have preserved that parish-feeling. But, he adds, most of them were Maltese, Italians and Portuguese who still had a bit of faith—at least a few habits and practices. Unfortunately, there are many others who do not even give a thought to Christian life and practices.

Is it not one of the consequences of our age's materialism that it so wraps man up in his work and his pleasure that they become his sole interest, his whole life? Such "worlds" become all the more impenetrable as they are cut off from the spirituality of the Church or of some broader ideal which could cut through the materialistic walls of his environment and unite him to his fellow man. Accordingly, we feel justified in drawing this conclusion: these segments of life and the means to reach them—means we must never disregard but study ever more attentively—indicate that the territorial concept of the parish must now be cast aside as powerless to evangelize the modern world.

We can never overestimate the force which groups exert upon the minds and the lives of individuals. It seems that life today is designed, like some frightful machine, to melt enormous blocs of society together. And among all those blocs the working class is the one that thinks most "collectively."

Of course, we should not exaggerate; oversimplification would make us forget even the elementary laws of psychology. Despite the pressure brought to bear upon them, thank God, human beings can still find satisfying outlets in this world of ours. Many people think and react according to the pattern prevalent where they work or go for relaxation. Many wait for the press or the radio to hand them ready-made opinions. On the other hand, many revert to their own personal way of thinking when they reach home, reacting quite differently now that they are with their family, friends and neighbors.

Family and neighborhood create two very real environments. Even in our day, every human being is indelibly marked by the family which formed him and the family which he forms. The influence of one's neighborhood, though generally harder to detect, is none the less sure. There are some districts where priests can be certain of a hearty welcome, and others where they are considered kill-joys; some where the young can remain good without too much trouble, others where it is almost impossible; some where Catholic youth organizations recruit members year after year, and others where never a worker can be found or a team formed; some where it is customary, though no less spontaneous, for the people to help each other, and some where it is just as customary to squabble.

But the family and the neighborhood are precisely the two spheres in which the parish can operate. The parish can act upon persons because it deals with them at every stage of their development within the family—childhood, adolescence and maturity; and it does so by influencing not only individuals but also the family, and,

in a more general way, the mentality of the neighborhood.

Indeed, the chief accomplishment of the parochial
apostolate today seems to be its influence upon the
home and the awakening of numerous small communities. As a result, the preaching of the word is no longer
confined to the pulpit and many more people benefit by
spiritual direction. The ideal of perfection is no longer
one of individual advancement. The leaven has been
put where it belongs. The parish priest now arouses and
assembles the community, starting from the basic cell
(which is the home), reaching the entire community
(which is the parish), and including all the other more
or less sporadic and enduring smaller communities
formed to answer some particular need. Eventually
these groups become centers whence good influences
radiate, and points where human personality is no
longer cramped but enabled to reach its full development, morally and spiritually as well as materially.

All these communities—and therefore the parish—
contact the individual exactly when he has the best
chance of shaking off the yoke of the collectivity and the
crippling weight of materialism. A man rediscovers
himself on coming home after a day's work. There he
finds his love, his cares, his personal problems; and if he
does not lend an ear to the religious question at that
time, he never will.

We should not, of course, foolishly imagine that
present-day wages, housing and home conditions are

ideal for the development of personality. In fact, the housing shortage is one of the worst social problems of our times. Still the fact remains that, in his own home and neighborhood, a man can draw deeper draughts of purer air. Family and neighborhood are the most fertile soil for the word of God—a fact which experience has pretty generally confirmed so far, especially with regard to the working class—and we must acknowledge that the best work, though slow and limited, has been done in these last few years and starting with the parish.

Though organizations like the *Jeunesse Ouvrière Catholique* have often tried to unite workingmen into groups, such groups have rarely seen the light of day and even more rarely lived through the night. It is difficult just to get the workers together before or after their day at the factory; even union meetings have the same problem. The proper psychological atmosphere is lacking. Militant Catholic Actionists can do much to improve those around them even while actually at work. But where shall they find the time and the means to replenish the springs of their activity? When and where shall new members be recruited if not during leisure time and in the little communities formed by the various "sections" outside of working hours?

The answer to those questions brings us to the role of the parish, since it is a fact that the most active and firmly established Catholic Action and Jocist teams are those which were created, nourished and sustained by parishes. Others, we might say, are rather more like

makeshifts and stopgaps—though God knows how
often and how badly they are needed because of shortcomings on the part of some parishes. As far as Catholic
Action is concerned, there are whole sections which resemble deserts and where some sort of federation is the
only thing that affords militant persons (often the self-
taught products of spontaneous generation) a chance to
work together and find for their spiritual life the nourishment their respective parishes cannot provide. Only
too often do we meet splendid Catholics, eager warriors
for Christ (conceived by some unaccountable power and
admirably trained by no one save the Holy Spirit), who
complain: "Our priests give us no encouragement whatever, no help at Sunday Mass, no solid food in their sermons, and no chance to meet with other parishioners."

Consider these all too common complaints, the pre-
carious existence of Catholic Action units which get
little or no support from the clergy, the lamentable deficiencies of parishes—consider all this and see whether
it does not prove that the harvest is ripe, the task urgent.

The *Jeunesse Ouvrière Catholique* has made astound-
ing progress since its earliest members first made themselves heard in the workman's world. Yet, we remind
ourselves of the resistance and the misunderstanding,
not to mention the contradiction often endured at the
hands of parish priests. We remember the many
branches set up haphazardly only to round off the list of
parish activities. We recall the sorrow apostles have expressed to us at not finding competent spiritual directors

in their home parish, and we wonder at the great work this movement might have accomplished had it come upon the atmosphere, the fertile soil and the priests it had a right to expect in every parish. We wonder at the scope it would have taken on, the good it could have done had each unit in each parish only been recognized and supported as a *real* unit. The sight of such magnificent results obtained despite a lack of co-operation from parishes makes us ask, not whether parishes can be effectual, but how very effectual they can be if only they do their job properly.

The working class seems an infrangible bloc, unfamiliar with the religious problem; and we can well repeat, like Cardinal Suhard, that it is cut off from the Church by a thick wall or, like Abbé Godin, that it is a vast mission field. For a pastor to think or say otherwise proves he has never dared look out from his bourgeois ivory tower or has systematically forgotten or deformed what he has seen.

All the same, we may say that a seven-league step has been taken since the start of the *Jeunesse Ouvrière Catholique* and that, being the first, it was the hardest step of all. No matter how arduous the work done by missionaries and how slow the progress made by the Church in subsequent years, it is always the first step— arriving in a country and setting up the first center of Catholicism—that is the most difficult.

Catholic Action in France may appear to have made little progress since 1927. It may not have spread far and wide but it certainly has struck its roots deep. Militant members have arisen just about everywhere. The genuine Christian may still be an exception in his shop but he is no longer an anomaly. This victory makes us look forward to greater victories to come. This first step proves that other steps can and will be taken. The only danger is, not that the reapers may become overconfident, but on the contrary that they may give up in despair. Here as elsewhere, people who work with constancy and enthusiasm have no illusions—illusions being nothing but the so-called realistic views of the bored or the impulsive, who value their work according to the quick and brilliant results they obtain.

Let each parish and each parish priest fully recognize his duties with regard to Catholic Action, especially toward the working class, and we shall soon see that the "illusions" of those who believe in it and in the parish are the least illusory of all.[2] We say "Catholic Action"

[2] We wish, however, to make this point clear: in attributing such efficacy to the parish, we are not in the least underestimating the need of action on a broader scale. We feel, instead, that the work done in any parish must go hand in hand with that done by regional and national organizations. Everything we said about the immense sectors of life and thought makes this necessary. Militant laymen should be able to get together in order to map out a course of action and present a united front. If they are to take part in other movements for the temporal betterment of mankind, they will need chaplains, appointed by the hierarchy, to help them do the work of the Church on every level and in every field. We have insisted that the parish is indispensable for the mustering and animating of militant mem-

and "parish" in the same breath because we insist that Catholic Action must receive its impetus from the parish and that both go together.

More than anything else, our age needs that every corner of it be illuminated by an authentic and broad-scaled witnessing to the gospel of Christ. Words persuade only insofar as they echo sincere conviction; example leads people on only if it is more than an external attitude. People distrust whatever smacks of propaganda, hypocrisy and self-interest.

Now, the plain truth is that in all the worlds which make up our modern world we do not see the leaven of the gospel exert its power. Moved and informed by other philosophies and dynamic concepts, they seem totally ignorant of Christian thought. The latter must be carried right to their very door, and the urgency of the task has given rise, of late, to any number of undertakings, some of which do the work of paratroopers behind the wall of materialism.

It would be ridiculous to expect immediate and tangible results from these undertakings. Asking a priest-worker whether he has seen the fruits of his chosen way of life is like pulling up newly planted shrubs every night to see whether they have taken root. Regardless of

---

bers, but we have not thereby lessened the need of other kinds of activity, for without them the activity of the parish would be sporadic and ineffectual.

the orientation and the scope given to such movements (as, for example, the *Mission Ouvrière* mentioned by the French hierarchy when asking the priest-workers to modify their program), we know very well that those movements will not be enough and will not take up all of a priest's energy and devotion.

To hear certain people talk, you would think that the parish ministry was something outmoded, something engaged in temporarily to satisfy diocesan authorities and performed without enthusiasm as if their real work lay elsewhere.

In this matter, too, rigidity can lead one into error. Why must apostles always feel they are contradicting one another whereas they are complementing one another? You would think that one undertaking immediately precluded all others and that everything was outdated because of a new discovery in the apostolate. Though a certain area is illuminated by a beacon, there may be obstacles within the area that cast shadows and therefore must be lit from behind. Even so, it is expedient and urgent that the light of the gospel be enkindled behind the wall which separates the working class from Christ and the Church.

What does that mean concretely? It means that those spheres which seem impervious to Revelation must be shown an authentic example of the Christian life which will teach them the value of that life and lead them to imitate it. It means, furthermore, that Christ must be introduced where His Church cannot be, that His gospel must be lived where He cannot be adored, and that a little charity must be practiced where the gospel cannot be preached in its entirety. But we should not forget that charity, the gospel, Christ and the Church are one and the same thing and that there can never be a genuine revelation without an explicit revelation of Christ and His Church.

Some cannot bear the full brightness of the light and others, in their search, do not think they can find it in the visible Church. Unfortunately, many of our most sincere contemporaries experience difficulty in seeing the fascinating Christ in the clergy; they find it hard to hear a faithful echo of the gospel in our Sunday sermons; and they have even more trouble recognizing modern parishes as the descendants of the early Christian communities.

Must we for that reason abolish all parishes, eliminate all sermons and dismiss all the clergy? Would it not, instead, be wiser and more expedient to restore to them their truly Christian savor? Revealing the Church means, not so much camouflaging it, but showing it as it ought to be and is in the mind of Christ, and making it what it should be.

Whether we like it or not, the Church, for our contemporaries, is the hierarchy and each parish church, together with those who run it and those who live around it. Especially of the crowds is it true that their contact with the Church is made through the parish; they see the Church and deal with it through the parish.

When they say "clergy," they mean the pastor and the
curates who work in their midst. When there is an official religious act to be performed, they go to their parish church. Whether arranging for baptism or the pub-
lication of marriage banns or enrolling their children in
a Christian doctrine class, they go to the sacristy or the
rectory. It may be a wedding or a funeral, but everything revolves around the parish church. Even the la-
borer who has been greatly impressed by the example of
a fellow workman or a priest-worker must some day
ring the rectory doorbell or assist at a church service.
Now, suppose he has been drawn there by the ideal of
the gospel and, coming in during the sermon, hears
nothing but a talk on money and collections. Suppose he
has been led on by his need for a sense of community
and finds only a shapeless, loosely knit group of worshipers at high Mass. Or suppose he has conceived a
lofty notion of Christian charity and is received in the
sacristy just as if it were a business office. If such things
happen, you may be sure that any lesson put across at
home or at work by priest or layman will be danger-
ously overshadowed by the almost official contradiction
met with at church.

It would be ridiculous, however, to make the parish's
function something purely negative when it, too, in
every phase of its life and activity, can bear glorious
witness to the gospel. Let a parish do away with class
consciousness and price-lists, for instance, and not only
will the faithful few be impressed by the change—they

may even be the last to appreciate it—but it will soon be the topic of conversation in every factory. To take another example: a young couple come to the rectory and make arrangements for their wedding. They cannot help thinking seriously of more important matters if the priest, instead of explaining a complex scale of rates for carpets, music and decorations, dwells primarily and exclusively on preparation for their entire married life. If Christians everywhere showed real brotherly love for one and all, and if it were a matter of course to find the spirit of Christ in cities or wherever there is a job to be done, a problem to be settled, or a cause to be supported, such examples of charity would not redound to the praise of one man's convictions and devotedness but would make people look to the very source of that general spirit.

For such witnessing to be genuine and effective in the world of today, it cannot be the work of a few. No, every single Catholic has to understand his duties toward the very life of society and react in every place and circumstance according to the doctrine of the gospels. Naturally, we have to make allowances for human weakness (and our contemporaries are quite understanding on that score), but until Christians as a whole see the necessity of Catholic Action there will be no worth while witnessing to the gospel and the Church will not be showing the world the true likeness of Christ. There are two alternatives: either everything that bears the name of Christian will live up to its ideal and thus enlighten the world, or it will fall short and sporadically flame and flicker.

Now, in our mind, the agency chiefly responsible for this united action is the parish; first, because the parish is the center where Catholics meet in a body, and then because the essential work of parish priests is to summon and sustain apostles.

From a purely utilitarian and even from a tactical viewpoint, the most elementary strategy requires that the apostolate depend upon the parish. We need paratroopers, as we have said; still in all, the spreading of the kingdom is the work of the masses. Though it is only too true that our good Catholics, as a whole, are often torpid, we should not declare them hopeless and accuse them of every crime. After all, they are people who have remained faithful to the Church, and, in our modern world, that fact alone bespeaks a certain amount of good will, moral stamina and love of Christ. Their stamina may not always have been well developed or properly oriented, but is that a reason to let it remain unused any longer? As soon as we make them want to act, they say, "Tell us what we should do." It would be better, no doubt, if they had enough initiative to discover it for themselves and knew how to reduce their ideal to practice; but it is none the less true that many of them are ready to give themselves unsparingly, to assist the clergy, to let their belief shine out over the world.

We must confess at the outset that the job is a tremendous one, bigger than all of us. Any priest who tries to stimulate souls to action, be they youths or whole families, soon gets a feeling of helplessness before the magnitude of the task and in no time exhausts his store of time and energy. No one can hope to influence more than a relatively small group of his fellow men; but the more a priest does, the more he finds to do—a fact which can easily make him flit from one thing to another or sink into discouragement. There can never be enough priests to fill the need and it would be a serious mistake, almost a heresy with regard to Catholic Action, if there were. Priests are not supposed to take the place of militant laymen but rather must they find and develop such laymen. Never numerous enough to be everywhere, priests must be posted at strategic points. But if in their parishes they act, not as administrators but as awakeners, they will find many souls who can apply their own limited activity to an indefinite number of concentric spheres. This work will progress slowly, and we will never live to see the masses converted. Actually, these masses are like a country which can be conquered only yard by yard. This does not mean, however, that the purely apostolic work inspired and guided by the parishes is less effective than the many paratrooping missions organized independently of any parish.

Moreover, conversion work, fascinating as it may be for any Catholic, is not the most urgent of our present duties. The important thing, as we have said, is that every Catholic should live his religion to the full. What

we need is mature lay Catholics, and not somewhat
childish ones who possess good will but are afraid to
move without orders from their pastor. But this again is
the lookout of the parish. Clearly, parishioners will remain immature just as long as pastors are content to
lead them from on high like almighty Jupiters. That
kind of leadership does not call for supermen; but to
develop initiative, to work with the whole parish as a
team, to remain in the background and let the parishioners assume their own responsibilities, that calls for real
leaders and not adjutants. Never will we have a mature
laity until our parishes have priests of this caliber in
tactical positions. To want to use them elsewhere is, in
our opinion, a grave mistake.

If the situation in a parish needs changing or improv-
ing, that is all the more reason for rallying around. The
transformation cannot be wrought by ignoring facts,
and even less can the job be entrusted to such as refuse
to see or change anything. This work is delicate, difficult, and it requires open minds and ready devotedness.
Must all the valor and dynamism of our young clergy
spend itself on projects and techniques that have nothing to recommend them but their newness, and cast
aside as unimportant the basic, essential work which
alone can keep them from building on sand?

The fact of the matter is that nowadays, when other
duties seem more spectacular and allow for no end of
versatility, parish work appears dull and definitely short
on glamor. And there is a lot of truth in this view, for,

as a priest once said to me, "It is easy to turn a cure into a sinecure." If a priest, however, realizes how much there is to be done, if he tirelessly studies ends and means, and concentrates on them without, for all that, closing his mind to new problems and methods, he will spend many a sleepless night and at death will doubtlessly bewail the fact that his work is still unfinished. The job of the parish priest is a difficult one, long-drawn-out and often monotonous. It takes patience and calls, not for such as love to draw up tidy reports and collect laurel wreaths, but for humble workers who have the will to tackle a tough job and do it well.

CHAPTER III

ALL THINGS TO ALL MEN

The inconstant are not drawn to parish work since, for reasons just explained, it is not their cup of tea.

A pastor does the work at hand as it is; or, more correctly, he does the work handed him to do, being at the disposition of superiors who send him where he is needed, not to work a while and move on, but to effect the slow but sure transformation of his parish.

His primary duty is to see the situation as it is, and not as he would want it to be. That constitutes his first major problem, for we all tend to call good what we wish to retain and bad what we can easily change. It is always a great temptation to say that our predecessor accomplished nothing and to strike out in exactly the opposite direction, as if to build ourselves a pedestal on the ruins of his work or to assert ourselves by discrediting him.

A pastor must see things as they are because he has no right to pick and choose only the jobs that suit him. He may prefer one aspect of the ministry—working with children or adolescents, for instance, or perhaps with adults. He may have a special liking for confession or an aptitude for preaching. He may be so drawn to the poor that if he listened to himself he would spend all his time visiting them and solving their problems. Perhaps he would rather work among the sick. Or again he may be ideally suited to serve as chaplain for some Catholic Action group. The truth is that all his qualifications can help him in the ministry but that he may not concentrate exclusively on any one of them or even be dominated by one.

A pastor must be able to do everything. He undertakes whatever task awaits him with all the attendant circumstances of person, time and place, and sees it through to the end without being carried away by whims or weighted down with weariness. He takes charge of children's summer schools, young people's sodalities, social clubs or family groups exactly as they are, since it is not he who has chosen them. He may find docile, devoted, intelligent workers in some quarters and only mediocre ones in others. Yet all of them have been entrusted to him in the same way and he does not know which ones the Lord will eventually call to be His chosen apostles. He is not dealing with hypothetical characters but with the real people God has placed in his care. His mission does not consist in forming or perfecting a splendid Catholic Action unit, but rather in tending the flock he finds in the pasture turned over to him.

Even though he does everything in his power for such

units, he should expect deceiving ups and downs and new difficulties each day. At any time he may encounter a youngster who shows signs of ill will, find that someone he was counting on has suddenly gone away, or sense some unaccountable hostility which may well undermine all his labors.

At certain moments, no doubt, he will have to assert his authority, yet his authority is not like that of an executive or even of a professor. He has no right to get rid of people, simply throwing them out because they bother him; and before deciding on such a course, he has to weigh the matter with infinite care.

No, the pastor cannot be a creature of whims. Neither can he put his work aside when it becomes tedious. Quite the contrary: he grows old with his flock and his heaviest cross often consists in seeing no improvement in it. How can he tell whether his efforts have borne fruit over the years? Some parishes make promising beginnings, but lasting success is no surer for all that. With time, they may seem ready to scale the heights. Still the shepherd of souls should not grow complacent or rest on his laurels. Instead, he must ever keep his eye on what has yet to be undertaken, perfected, transformed.

Only those who have been engaged in parish work can appreciate what it is to have heart and soul constantly whipped and crucified by the problems it poses. To get some idea of their difficulties, we need only try to imagine the details connected with merely visiting the sick or with planning a feast which will draw the crowds and have missionary significance. Is it surprising, then, that at times priests are sorely tempted to turn to some type of work that allows for more freedom and variety?

And yet is there a more eminently priestly work than this? The pastor does not choose what he wants to do; he has to do everything.

He is an educator, but his pupils represent every social condition and all ages—children, adolescents and especially adults. By "children" we mean all the children in the parish, the children of common laborers as well as those of the rich. And by "adults" we mean, not a group, but all of them as far as possible, individually or collectively, directly or indirectly.

In his parish the priest is specifically a teacher of spirituality. He can be an educator even though he does not spend the better part of each day teaching some science or secular art; in fact, the more he endeavors to work on a spiritual plane, the better he will accomplish his task. Without pretense he can be a religious educator his whole life long; for he is a priest, and solely a priest.

He may have a special love for the poor. Well, they will not be lacking in any parish—all kinds of them: those who come to the rectory, the real poor or the professional beggars (and how poor *they* are!), and those who will not come and whose plight you have to guess and relieve secretly.

Could such a priest possibly dream of devoting his life to relief work? If he did, he would have to choose one type of case and specialize in it; then if someone came who did not fit into his particular line of work, he would have to say, "Sorry, but we can't do anything for you." One day in the sacristy will prove to anyone that each parish presents every possible kind of problem. Then there are strikes, shutdowns and housing shortages, and, above all, those unforeseen, exceptional cases which are always the most tragic and the hardest to solve. Such is the lot of every priest who keeps both his heart and his eyes open.

We have not mentioned the spiritually poor, and yet how often parish priests hear people say, "I don't go to church and I have no faith; still I come to see you and I tell you things I couldn't tell anyone else."

More than any other priest the shepherd of souls has to be a preacher of the word. It is impossible to overestimate the power of sermons when pastor and curates take pains to make them instructive, timely and appealing. The vitality of a parish, as well as the inspiration given Catholic Actionists and the nourishment afforded the spiritual life of all the faithful, depends to a large extent on the quality of the preaching done there. To communicate the life in the word of life, the pastor and his assistants must know how to speak and hold the interest of their listeners. In passing, we should like to say that any priest can learn to deliver interesting and worth while sermons if only he works and practices in collaboration with his fellow priests. But that subject would lead us too far afield.

The parish priest, more than any other, must be a preacher and a good one. Unlike professional speakers, he is beset by this difficulty: he has to preach every Sunday, on every feast, and at every meeting held in the parish. Though he has been rehashing his sermon outlines for the past five or ten years, he must continue doing so not only because someone may remember them but because there is so much to say and because time and the human mind march on. He cannot repeat; rather, he must ever renew his matter and his manner of presenting it. Practice should make him perfect but not give him that glibness which turns sermons into a wearisome waste of time and makes parishioners very clever at avoiding them. On the other hand, if his sermons are vital and make demands on the congregation, you will find everyone in the parish telling his neighbor he considers them an integral part of his week and could not get along without them.

Who can deliver a more effective sermon than a shepherd of souls? Who is in a better position than he to know his hearers, their needs and reactions, to know what he should say and how he should say it? Is there any other preacher who can follow his charges as closely as he in the progress they make and the changes they undergo, through all their anxieties, their temporal and

spiritual cares? No one, therefore, is better qualified to
talk their language and be understood by them, to teach
them how to react and embody spiritual values in their
whole life. But that requires observation, thought,
work, and it is a difficult job.

We hope no one will be surprised to hear us say that
the parish priest is, more than anyone, a chaplain for
Catholic Action units. We have already said how indispensable the parish is for the functioning and progress
of Catholic Action. We may go further and state that it
is the very source of Catholic Action. What do we mean
when we say that the pastor has been entrusted with the
care of souls? We mean it is his mission to enkindle the
Christian spirit in everyone confided to him. And that
he can best do by making his parishioners conscious of
their responsibilities. For too long now we have nar-
rowed those responsibilities down to individual prayer
and personal morality. But in this age, when everything
takes on a social and cosmic meaning, Catholics have to
work together at common tasks; and it is doubtlessly because preceding generations failed to do so that they al-
lowed the world to grow pagan in every sphere. A Catholic is not someone who goes to church on Sunday and
receives at Easter, contributes to the support of the
Church and marches in all the processions. A Catholic is
someone who, everywhere and in all circumstances,
strives to live according to the gospel. A Catholic is
someone who loves Christ, is proud of Him, wants Him
to be known and loved, and tries to establish His king-

dom of love throughout the world. Now, people do not think of these things spontaneously or, if they do, they soon forget them in the rush of egoism and daily living. But that is precisely where the pastor can do something; for he is the mandated spiritual director of his entire parish. As such, it is his duty to preach the gospel in season and out—not some vague, impractical gospel but one suited to the concrete circumstances of twentieth-century life; it is his duty to reprove, to denounce the sin of the world, and preach a crusade against it. What does that mean, practically, if not the conversion of Catholics into militant Catholic Actionists? We try to get apostles, not because we want to keep Catholic Action alive and growing, but because all Christians are called to be soldiers of Christ and have to answer that call. Where are those Christians? And who is in such daily contact with them, who knows them as well, visits and follows them as closely, and is as solicitous for their perfection as their pastor? If he fails to inspire and sustain them, those who have to do so in his stead can only fill the deficiency as well as contacts and circumstances allow. Pastors and curates are the only ones to do this work and until they do it, specialized Catholic Action will not reach its full stature, Christians will be unchristian, the dough will fall flat, the Church will not really be the Church.

More than any other priest, the parish priest is a chaplain of specialized Catholic Action—not only in one place but everywhere. In a parish where there are

several curates, one may devote himself especially to
workers, another to key men, and so on; yet in the sector
entrusted to him each priest meets people from every
rank and walk of life. In any case, parish work as a
whole—the full mission of the priest—embraces each
and every milieu, so that the shepherd of souls is, so to
speak, a chaplain whose specialty is Everyman.

Here again his task is a hard one because it lies in a
field which has yet to be tilled. Unless he is a realist, he
will fail, since obedience to reality is the basic law of
successful Catholic Action. That law applies to the level
of organization which we may call Catholic Action
units. But the parish is anterior to the unit, for it is there
like a fertile field even before a unit has sprung up. The
chaplain of a unit may find it already formed; but the
parish priest finds only the field which his parish is, and,
even when a unit already exists, the rest of the parish
still stretches all about him like a vast fallow-ground.
He cannot stop once a unit has been set up; he must
keep on until the whole parish has become a body of
specialized Catholic Action. Now, this field to be
plowed and sown—that is reality, the reality whose
laws, and whims sometimes, he must know and love or
miserably fail.

And now for a remark made with malice toward
none. A national director can launch new ideas, propose
novel techniques, and suggest goals as fast as he dreams
them up; and if he is clever at all, he will usually find
enough enthusiastic followers throughout the country

to put his ideas into practice. Needless to say, we cannot recommend such procedures to a national director. The parish priest, on the other hand, need not even be warned against them. If he has illusions, cold facts will soon make him come down to earth in spite of himself. He cannot move without contemplating his parishioners and asking himself what he has to work with, what sort of people they are, what they have to offer, and what they can do. Let him act otherwise, and he will fail.

The very factors which make parish work long and hard also guarantee its effectiveness. Here the demands made upon a priest betoken success. His task is difficult because it leaves no room for fancy; and it leaves no room for fancy because he must perform it, not in the clouds or in the realm of abstract thought, but in the midst of the most objective, immediate and gripping reality.

Time is no respecter of things wrought without regard for it, whereas those done in accordance with its laws are likely to be solid and lasting achievements. The fundamental rule for parish ministry is: Know and be known. Christ puts it even more plainly when describing the Good Shepherd: "I know mine and mine know me." Mutual knowledge of this sort takes time, grows ever more intimate and is never over; the deeper it is, the more possibilities it offers.

The shepherd knows his sheep. In a rural parish the pastor can get around to visiting every family in a few months' time. He soon recognizes every face and even

starts to sense the sympathy, indifference or hostility
hidden behind it. Still his knowledge will grow with
the months and the years. Gradually he comes to know
every family's problems for having heard about them or
having been asked to help solve them. He becomes familiar with the difficulties of individuals too. Of course,
many mysteries will never be explained to him, but no
priest can spend years among his people without learning the story of this or that family, this or that piece of
good or ill fortune. Over the years, he not only knows
but lives out everyone's story. There is always one generation he baptized, one he prepared for first Communion and others which are growing old and passing on.
The longer he lives, the more he knows and the more
everyone realizes it. He knows his parish and his parishioners.

A city pastor, on the contrary, cannot get to know
everyone. There are many people of whose names and
existence he must ever remain ignorant. In large suburban or city parishes the majority will be strangers to
him, and broad areas of life and thought will escape
him. That is a fact he must face but never cease to bewail. Yet, who can know this multitude better than he
—or better than they, since priests work together as a
team? Every day a priest meets more families and receives new callers. With each priest exploring on his
own the area assigned to him, entire districts are eventually discovered, and, if not wholly illuminated, at least
brought within the range of the Light. Each priest can

then acquaint his team mates with what he has learned and those he has met, though it is by no means necessary for each single priest to know everything and everyone personally. As was stated earlier, the "shepherd of souls" is not only the pastor or the curates but all of them together, and it is essential that the *collective* shepherd have a true and vital concept of what his parish is.

Finally, the city priest, almost as well as his brother in the country, comes to know the reactions of his flock. He bears them within himself and lives them, lives their life. He senses what has to be said or left unsaid. He realizes that he can count on some and must be wary of others. He foresees the possible results of what he says and undertakes. Not only can he preach or preside over a meeting without being advised, but if he has any tact and experience he knows spontaneously how best to get his message across. He is ever mindful of his parishioners, their way of life, their likes and dislikes. He speaks their language and has a better chance of being understood. Seen in the right light, this knowledge appears, not as another new technique, but as a source of power hard to overestimate.

The shepherd of souls knows his sheep and his sheep know him. In the rectory or the sacristy, the church or the street, the priest is at the disposition of the faithful from morning till night. He should be and he is always available, and that is how most people think of him. At first even this idea of him is superficial, but gradually it grows deeper as circumstances justify it. People who come to see him find him gracious. They feel that here is someone who is trying to understand their problems, someone who bears their burden with them. They tell him not only their spiritual difficulties but all sorts of worries and cares. They notice that he listens, thinks, answers and, over and above answering, takes matters in hand as much as he can, sheds light in darkness, and takes the necessary steps to remedy a situation.

If he does these things, the entire flock will soon know its shepherd, for those who know him will be telling others about him. Slowly but surely he becomes a figure in the eyes of his parishioners. And that is where he can give his most telling testimony; that is where he must reproduce as closely as possible the likeness of Christ—good, understanding, gentle and firm at the same time. "It's a great thing to have a good priest in a district," a peasant once said to me while describing the local pastor in a voice full of admiration for his genuinely priestly ministry.

People do not ask their pastor to be an intellectual giant, a brilliant organizer or an intrepid fighter. No, they want him to be first and foremost—and exclusively —a priest. Even those who approach him for material assistance pay special note to the way he receives them. Though their business be secular, what they are looking for is the charity of Christ. Let us not forget that the priest, more than anyone else, is considered the witness par excellence to the Church. For all practical purposes we can say that in the mind of the faithful he and his fellow priests *are* the Church.

It may be objected that we have painted too idealized a picture of the country priest, and indeed the situation in densely populated suburbs is not as romantically perfect as sometimes pictured. When you consider a priest in any large city, you are struck first of all, not by the thought that he is well known, but rather that hardly anyone can possibly know him. Still, as we have pointed out, that priest is not one man; he is part of a team, and we should not undervalue the power of it.

In this matter of "learning" a parish, teamwork is a process of multiplication, not mere addition. What matters far more than the sum of the findings of individual priests is the views of the team, its ideas, and its joint efforts. If they are the product of constant co-operation, those views will be doubly sound, those ideas broader and deeper, those efforts more pertinent and effective. Far from being a mere research group, a team of this kind is a cell living in the midst of the faithful, trying to understand their reactions better, checking and correcting their opinions. It is, furthermore, a smaller and more earnest community which prays at the center of that larger community, the parish. We must not think of it as a committee studying problems of sociology or psychology. To put the matter briefly, a team is a single soul, a single heart, trying to beat and live in unison with the parish. It is a source of power, and of power that has not yet been guessed.

A team, moreover, consists not only in a group of priests but soon includes those who, in their own small or big way, regularly or intermittently, take part in the parish apostolate. When clergy and laity join forces to study their parish, it is obvious how greatly the laity can help. It will supply names, addresses and personal information, but especially it will express viewpoints and value judgments closely bound up with everyday life. As the priestly team keeps doing its work, the lay half of the team takes shape, adheres to it, encircles and grows with it.

Time is the big factor here. No passing force can ever have the impact of a team knit more closely together with every day. Our failure to appreciate this reservoir of strength has kept us from getting the best out of our parishes. As a result, they have lost their vigor and paralysis has set in. A parish has many means of carrying on its apostolate, all of which work better the more we know about men and their environment; and if only we realize this fact, we can then gauge the possibilities of the basic means.

Of those means we should like to list just a few. The pastor has at his disposal a pulpit and a congregation which he does not have to call together; and since he knows his sheep, it depends entirely upon him whether he will or will not be heard. By "pulpit" we mean not only his preaching of sermons but his teaching of catechism classes attended by many or most of the children in the parish. There is no generation which he does not influence. God alone knows how often he can reach parents through their children if only he knows how to make the most of every opportunity. The pulpit, again, is the remarks he makes at every meeting. It is the parish bulletin and all types of publications.

In addition, we could mention the many societies and organizations, social and charitable, which have sprung up in the last few decades. These groups and undertakings represent many different corners of the parish. Granted that they have developed rather haphazardly, they are none the less a striking proof of all the human and material resources the parish holds. And, we repeat, if they were seconded by a thorough knowledge of the people and their environment, many withered branches would doubtlessly have to be left for the fire, but ever so many more could be given a new life and made to bear fruit.

One glance at this wealth of material, moral and spiritual resources, and we need no longer ask ourselves, "Is there anything the parish can do?" but rather, "Why isn't it doing more?"

No nation-wide movement and no political party can boast of so many supporters from all quarters, so many enthusiasts totally dedicated to their cause (we are thinking, for example, of all the nuns who assist parish priests), or such a variety of ways and means as can that nation's parishes as a whole. What we lack is, not possibilities and methods, but men—men with enough zeal to care and work without ceasing, men with enough hu-

mility to face the facts and see each problem as it really
is, men who are so united with God that it is always He
who is working through them. With such men in a parish, we no longer have to worry about it: it will march
on confidently, progress and discover new possibilities
at every turn.

We do not realize how much could be accomplished
by parish work if it were always genuine parish work.

CHAPTER IV

THE SONS OF CHARITY

History shows us that the religious life has been of extraordinary benefit to the Church.

Some consider the religious life as a means of enhancing their priestly consecration, of stabilizing their spiritual life or of enlarging the scope of their apostolate. Some deem it an ideal in itself. But in dedicating themselves both groups are seeking the glory of God. By utterly surrendering their heart and their will, all that they are and all that they have, they are saying, "Lord, this one act is the homage we want to offer You, by our whole life and the use we make of it, for our life and everything You have given us."

Consecrating oneself to God means undergoing a long and arduous preparation in order to attain a peak of fervor and then trying to remain there, adjusting one's whole life to that level—burning one's bridges behind one, in a manner of speaking, so as to find oneself stripped of everything and locked in the arms of God.

That is the goal of the religious life. It is what everyone on profession day wants to reach, somehow or other.

For examples of bridge burning consider the hermits who went into the desert to live a life of contemplation, the monks who surrender their will into the hands of their abbot, and the girls who shut themselves off from the world behind cloister and grille. Freed thus from the temptation of going back on their word, they can try to keep their eyes fixed on God alone.

Though the religious life was at first contemplative, over the years this perfect consecration to the service of God came to be prized as a marvelous instrument in the service of the Church. As urgent and difficult, not to say heroic, tasks confronted them, men of good will understood that those very tasks could be a means of consecrating themselves to God. They knew such work required dogged perseverance and not just a short-lived enthusiasm, and they saw that the religious life was their best guarantee of steadfastness.

If people can renounce the world to give themselves up wholly to contemplation, why can they not push fear aside to ransom captives, leave their family to evangelize the natives of far-off countries, and forget their comfort when duty bids them assist the poor? Whenever zeal and charity have found a new objective, it has become a means of asceticism for souls who wanted to give themselves completely to Christ. In this way the religious life offered its followers a chance to serve God and neighbor and to consecrate themselves entirely to His glory, at the same time spreading that glory throughout the world and practicing in every detail of

daily life the twofold commandment "Thou shalt love
the Lord thy God with thy whole strength, and thy
neighbor as thyself for the love of God."

Nowadays no one who longs for the extension of
God's kingdom can help being preoccupied with the tremendous problems presented by the evangelizing of the
working class. It is like a vast untilled field: the further
we walk through it, the more we realize how much must
be done before it can be reclaimed.

For many years now, excessive industrialization has
been making throngs move from the country to the city.
Every year villages are deserted and whole generations
are swallowed up by the suburbs of large manufactur-
ing centers. Just as these droves come to offer their
physical and intellectual assets to industry, so must
others from among them also look toward the city and
follow them there to live among them as the priests
they will need.

Bringing the gospel to the masses is an enormous and
difficult job. And now is the hour when a specialized
body must rise up within the Church and be dedicated
by vocation and vow to the evangelizing of the working
class.

Young men in the Middle Ages dreamed of combin-
ing the life of a religious with that of a knight and
dying on the battlefield in the service of God. How,
then, can the youth of today help wanting to unite the
service of God and the service of their fellow men, the
love of the Church and the love of the working class?

The crying need of the times must make them decide to
live a life of poverty like their working brethren; they
must make that poverty the substance of their religious
asceticism and the pledge of their dedication to the
evangelizing of the modern world.

To be ever more truly priests, they should put aside
everything that could assure them an easy life, comfort,
success and promotions; and, having done so, they
might join a religious family and devote themselves for
good and all to the exclusive apostolate of the workingman. For, surely, young men called to the priesthood
may aspire to linking their whole life and future to the
fate of the working class. And, surely, in view of such a
gigantic and thankless task, that could be the goal of
a normal congregation within the Church.

The truth is that more and more aspirants to the
priesthood yearn solely to bring the gospel to the working class. Never before have they seen the multitude of
problems involved so clearly or desired so vehemently
to solve them. Yet the very number and variety of jobs
to be done presents a danger. There is so much to catch
their eye that, guided by their own likes and dislikes,
they may choose their own mission. Vocation and mission, however, are two different things. God calls a person, and, so that he may know he is called, gives him
certain signs, such as attraction, aptitudes and circumstances, which mean something only when evaluated
and accepted by proper ecclesiastical authority. It remains true, of course, that a vocation is detected to a

great extent by the person who hears the call. Once he has heard it, furthermore, he can answer it or not at his own risk.

Not so a mission. No one assumes a mission; he receives it. He may have a chance to ask for one, but the task he is doing becomes a mission only when he is sent, only when he has received his orders. Normally, he has a vocation first and receives a mission later, and the mission often makes the vocation more specific by concretizing it. When a person realizes he has a missionary vocation, he feels that he has been called someday to receive a definite mission in an area which has never had the faith or has lost it. Going to the ecclesiastical authority in that area, he says, "Here I am. I am ready to receive a mission from you in your territory."

To repeat, it is only natural that many young men today should want to volunteer for all the tasks and missions which the evangelizing of the working class entails. It is only natural, too, that the Church should see a specialized body rise up within itself wholly devoted to parish work, and to parish work among the laboring class.

His awareness of present-day needs and the desire for some form of real religious life led Père Anizan to conceive the idea of the Congregation of the Sons of Charity. His dream was to combine parish life and religious life, to practice poverty by living among the poor and the workers, to spend himself in the service of God by spending himself in his priestly ministry. With the intuition of a genius and thanks to his long experience in the apostolate, he understood the primacy and the efficacy of priestly work. Sensing the high mysticism and the essential realism of the twofold vocation, he invited his followers to live the life of pastors and curates within the framework of the religious life.

It is easy to see all the advantages to be derived from such a specialized group entirely given over to its particular work; from a body of men recruited from all corners and every walk and station in life, and united by the wish, the will, to do the same vital work.

When they meet, they do not have to start a conversation. They pursue the one which began in the soul of their founder and in their own soul when first they glimpsed the task that lay ahead of them. At each meeting they only go on with the same dialogue. Strangers yesterday, they speak the same language today. They are now united into one family by a common denominator, by the same spirit; and the variety of their temperaments, characters and qualifications will only increase the value of their common resources.

Everything helps to unify their efforts. Their ascetical life and their studies are cut out for them by their mission and their ministry. When the time comes for some to specialize—and it will come—they will be guided, not by personal preferences and momentary interest or weariness, but by their own fitness as judged by their fellow workers and especially by their superiors in view of the needs of the group.

The decisive factor is the work to be done rather than a liking for it. You join a religious community so that its work may be done and not so that you may have the pleasure of doing it yourself. You join a missionary society so that the missionary work may be accomplished and not so that you may give yourself a mission. It is the same with a young woman who enters a nursing congregation: she comes that the sick may be cared for, not necessarily that she may care for them herself. The only thing that matters is the work itself. You come only to lose yourself in it, to give yourself to it body and soul. You are not looking for success or personal satisfaction, but you are irresistibly drawn on by every challenge the times offer. The work may rack and drive you mercilessly. You may be judged a worthless instrument and even cast aside. More exactly, you will be lost in the mass of workingmen and never ask yourself what you may get out of it all. The main concern is that the harvest be plentiful and that each reaper work hand in hand with his companions and not worry about getting credit for the bit he does.

In view of their special qualifications, efficient organization may make secretaries or treasurers out of a young girl who yearned to nurse the sick and a young man who dreamed of converting the natives in some distant land. They must, therefore, be convinced that that is how they can best carry on the work in their own humble way. Joining a religious institute dedicated to the apostolate of the poor and the working class does not automatically mean a man will take over the job of Christianizing a certain neighborhood or pioneer a new phase of endeavor. But it does grant him the far more comforting guarantee that he will share, anonymously and selflessly, in a much broader realization of the general goal.

The various members of such a congregation can meet on common ground and help one another because they share the same views, but especially because they are united by their religious profession and must strive every day of their lives to attain their ideal, not by means of abstract ideas or emotional contemplation, but by a pooling of all their energy and labors.

A specialized body of this type will have to study the problems that stand in its way. That calls for meetings, for discussions and teamwork both within the parish and within the bigger team constituted by such a religious society. Thus will everyone benefit from the knowledge and initiative of individuals. Inspired as it is by their deep and undivided devotion to their work—the parish and the apostolate of the workingman—their specialization will be highly effective and proof against the dangers it might otherwise contain.

The amazing power of a religious congregation comes from the fact that its members, who join it in the springtime of life, are constantly shielded against the desire to take back their offering, conscious that they are not laboring alone but are backed up by other men who have consecrated themselves to work for the Lord with the same fervor and tenacity of purpose.

Many a young man who wants to become a priest and is considering parish work balks at what he sees around him. It may be a country pastor who has lived so close (in one sense) to his people that he is now nothing but a rustic himself. The only difference is that he says Sunday Mass. Apart from that, his bees and his garden get as much attention as the spiritual welfare of his parishioners. Again, it may be a city pastor who has an easy time of it, free from care and snugly ensconced in the lap of ease—if not of luxury. How can the plight of the poor and the workingman ever break through the walls of his ivory tower and touch him? Parish life as lived by certain priests seems altogether too comfortable and business-like.

"Since we are giving up the world and consecrating ourselves to God, let us do so as wholeheartedly and generously as we can." These words of Emile Anizan's on leaving home voice the sentiments of so many young men on the threshold of the priesthood. They want to give their life up to God—but not so as to take it back or let it become sclerotic, not so as to enjoy the comfortable life their priesthood may eventually afford them. Consequently, they are afraid of parish work. Unwilling to become "pastors"—and the word as they use it has a pejorative meaning—they shun parish work even though they realize it is the most important of all.

At any price they want to avoid the pitfalls into which they have seen others disappear.

The truth is, and we must admit it, that the parochial ministry as generally conceived and carried out today holds some real dangers. Naturally, they are not inherent to that ministry, and, thanks be to God, many priests manage to overcome them and live as true priests and apostles in their parish.

Let us, however, be realistic. Isolation, a sort of sclerosis, the acquiring of a bourgeois mentality, routine and the more unfortunate effects of growing old all appear on such a large scale and cramp so many priestly lives as to seem the result, not of personal shortcomings, but of general laws. We may liken them to a set of circumstances which eventually win out over the best of intentions.

Consider a young curate who has spent himself unstintingly for three or four years, always finding the days too short to answer the endless demands his work made upon him. When suddenly named pastor of a rural parish, can he help looking with fear upon the isolation in store for him? From now on, he will be alone day in and day out; alone to think, to feel, to plan and undertake everything; alone in those inevitable moments of weariness; alone to pray in his church through the week; alone in his parish, since there is no one in whom he can really confide and the nearest priest is

miles away. Too often the years spent in this solitude
will wall him in a shell which his enthusiasm and gen-
erosity cannot break through. After ten years or so in
country parishes, too many priests look back upon their
dreams of long ago and feel like calling them illusions.
Fortunately, teams have been organized in many dean-
eries and frequent conferences help to save the situation.

It is our fervent wish that the young priests who long
for community life and teamwork may keep that long-
ing alive till the end and be ever on the lookout to
make their dream an actuality. We could hope too that
the element of chance in the assignment of priests to
various parishes might not dissolve existing teams or
preclude fruitful meetings.

At first glance, there would seem to be less danger of
isolation in the city, but the facts prove otherwise. Let
us not even mention those priests who live quite alone
in their quarters. We can only wonder at how completely the idea of the priestly community—as it existed
in the days of Saint Augustine, for example—has been
lost in the course of the centuries.

Isolation is a real threat even to priests who share the
same life, gather around the same table and live under
the same roof; for what we should fear most is, not
physical or spatial, but moral isolation. Though they
live together and work in the very same vineyard, many
priests get so that they never discuss anything serious or
exchange views on spirituality or the apostolate. Under

such conditions, they almost necessarily lose their savor
and their dynamism, and they surely lack the prodigious
power they would derive from the backing up of a team.

On the other hand, mere membership in a religious
congregation does not shield a priest from moral isolation. Neither does profession automatically immunize
him to all the defects, the selfishness and the pride
which may plague him later. Kneeling together on the
same kneelers, hearkening to the same bell and calling
themselves brothers is no guarantee that a group of
men will share one dream, live the same spiritual life
and work together. Nevertheless, it is true that, from its
very foundation, every religious family and institute is
haunted by a desire for the ever closer brotherhood and
unity that come from sharing not only material posses-
sions but also those gifts of mind and heart which God
bestows on everyone. And until that community of life
is achieved, their dream torments them and stands before them as a reproach.

Though past generations may not have understood
this ideal of community life or seen the need of it, it
seems that the younger men of today cannot ignore it
and will find no rest till they have achieved it. In assigning pastor and assistants to a given parish a bishop may
be thinking only of putting the right man in the right
place, whereas the prime concern of a religious superior
is to insure harmony among his subjects. Of course, he
too can place his priests where they are most needed,

but he should never forget his duty of making "one single, loving family," as Père Anizan said, out of the communities committed to his care.

Now more than ever before, our young men are afraid of becoming bourgeois. And they have reason to be, since the temptation and the opportunity to settle for stuffy security dogs priests at every step. Rectories are often among the most comfortable and well-appointed houses in the neighborhood. Young curates start by buying a desk and often go on to fill their rooms with easy chairs, ottomans and knick-knacks, and sometimes with the kind of furniture you would expect to find in the home of a dowager.

The collections in certain parishes are quite gratifying—so much so that a priest may be tempted to set his heart on those parishes, and, once there, to benefit by the collections. Then, too, there are many ways of making people offer one a gift. We all know of such priests who live a life of great ease and lack nothing.[1]

[1] We would not forget the many priests—pastors and curates, in the country and in the city—for whom the material side of life is a serious and harassing problem. Many of them have to do without a housekeeper because they can neither pay nor feed her. They live a life of poverty harder than religious know, a life that crucifies them day after day. Missionary priests sometimes come to a dechristianized parish and ask for the pastor only to be told, "He must be at the rectory. We haven't seen him for quite a while." On reaching the run-down, deserted-looking rectory, they knock and, receiving no answer, walk into

Despite everything we have said about it, there is something worse than this bourgeois love of comfort and material well-being. Indeed, it is often a sign of bourgeois attitude of heart. Priests who used to have time for all their parishioners soon find it pleasanter to chat with the more cultured and educated, and much more enjoyable to deal with the well-to-do than with the poor of the working class. Eventually, they keep state or at least draw an enchanted circle within which they practice their ministry.

Never would they have consented to such a state of affairs in the beginning, but they soon found a host of good reasons and excuses to justify attitudes that would have shocked them a few years before. Aided and abetted by weariness and their new-found "wisdom," they spend their time on whatever is easiest and most eye-catching in the ministry. They represent the bourgeois priest at his worst.

Religious poverty has been defined as the certitude of never lacking anything, and there is perhaps as much truth in the definition as there is danger attached to the vow. Freedom from worry about shelter and food and clothing may very well be an evangelical ideal, but it

---

an empty room where piles of cans and jars are the only sign of life. In the next room they find the pastor sick in bed, too sick to get up and tell someone and too completely forgotten for anyone to inquire. He has been living alone for years. The cans and jars all about hint at his poverty and solitude. No religious congregation knows such cold, stark poverty as this.

can also be an unmistakable effect of laziness and egoism. Never having given a thought to material problems throughout his adult life, a religious may too
easily forget how vexing such problems are to those who
must wrestle with them.[2]

It is none the less true that all his life long poverty
curbs the desires of a faithful religious and keeps him
from making miserly calculations and setting something aside for a rainy day. We would find it hard to
appreciate the freedom he enjoys in his every thought
and deed from the simple fact that he never has to make
provision for illness or old age. Should someone in a
community be tempted to make things too cozy for himself, he is soon deterred by the superior and especially
by his brethren. Should that someone be the superior
himself—one who tends to ease the rules and makes life
too comfortable—he can be stopped by the ideal that
burns in the hearts of his subjects, for even the young
religious have their say in the community chapter and
are always there to cry out and keep the common will
from growing slack.

Priests may be bothered by other temptations, more
personal, more painful, and far more perilous. The life
of many a priest has been utterly ruined by some lapse

[2] The danger is far less serious for pastors and curates because
of their familiarity with all phases of parish work.

which came as a complete surprise in view of his past record and his present attitude. When a subdeacon offers himself to God, he gives himself with all the ardor of his young heart and is quite convinced he will be faithful to the end. He knows trials and temptations will assail him, but he trusts that with God's grace he may keep his word. Yet, how can he be sure that his bright hope, his fervor and the profound peace which his will and God's grace have wrought will last forever?

Sooner or later there are periods when one's interior life grows weak, when it may even sink temporarily into a dangerous lethargy. When the love of God wanes in one's heart, other loves creep in and claim it for themselves. Fatigue, too, harassing ministerial worries and late hours poring over problems set one's nerves on edge. Then again there are hours of discouragement, weariness and all sorts of trials. At such times a thoughtless word or action can be like the pebble which falls into a placid pool and breaks its surface into ever-widening waves of agitation. One unhappy word, spoken or heard, and the priest's heart feels its peace give way to a profound restlessness which will not be stilled. Sometimes temptation pounces upon him suddenly and brutally. Sometimes it gains admittance into his heart imperceptibly; and that is especially true of someone engaged in the care of souls, since his life is sedentary and consists largely of visits made or received. If weariness or spiritual anemia have deadened his will, he may wake up too late. At times, temptation comes from without, and it may be that his will is not strong enough to resist.

As could be expected, solitude, one of the worst temptations in its own right, only makes matters worse. In the dark night of isolation certain heartaches become too big to fight. At times one lacks the will and the strength to go seek help, or one loses all hope of finding it. And here again it will often be too late when one realizes the danger or, in a burst of energy, tries to clutch at some weapon to ward it off.

It is an incontestable fact that in these matters religious profession is no magic wand. The vow does not confirm a soul in virtue for good and all. On the other hand, religious life affords one an atmosphere, bounds, a superior and brethren, and these are most important in the hour of temptation.

Until the very end the framework of the religious life protects one imperceptibly against one's own weakness. Negatively, it offsets all manner of dangers. Positively, the whole spirit of a religious house helps by sustaining one's fervor. Sometimes, however, that is not enough, and there is no use pretending it is. In that case superior and brethren are an inestimable help. Take the superior, for instance. He is not just a pastor. Besides seeing to it that his parish functions properly, he must remember that his assistants are his sons and that he is largely responsible for their welfare. Then take one's fellow religious. The warmth that pervades a family is

still one of the greatest safeguards against temptations
of mind and heart. The very casualness and informality
of brethren rubbing elbows day in and day out is a protection and a bulwark.

Some may smile and shrug their shoulders at these
exterior means; some braggarts may rush into danger,
sure they will emerge unscathed. But we do not think
any priest's work has ever been seriously hindered by
the use of such safeguards, whereas we do know that
much good work has been definitely compromised because these helps, these supports, were not available or
had been cast aside.

Should a priest fall into sin—and, alas! it is possible
—the family we call a religious congregation proves an
incomparably simple, immediate and sure means of salvation. A court-like or purely administrative approach
to his plight could frighten him. Difficult as it may be,
a conversation between superior and subject will always
be that of father and son; whatever is said, the solution
to the problem will be as merciful and efficacious as
possible and their interview will end on a note of re-
conciliation and encouragement. We can hardly refrain
from mentioning cases where priests might have been
lost forever had not a single confidential talk with their
superior put them back on the right road.

Besides isolation and discouragement, which are dangerous because they are temptations, there is another

danger which is not a temptation but a law common to all men. We refer to growing old. All of us age imperceptibly. With every day we lose some of our physical energy, notice it and tell others; our minds grow duller and dimmer too, but we notice it less and tell no one. Our best qualities—versatility, courage, initiative—give way to a sort of unconscious complacency at the sight of our achievements and of traditional ways of acting. For prudence we substitute timidity.

No one can escape this law. We need only look around to see how many parishes suffer from the effects of it. Once active and enterprising but now short-winded, many a pastor ends by suffocating the parish into which he had once breathed life.

What can be done about it? Canon Law says that the pastor of any parish, whether in Christian or in pagan lands, is irremovable. Unless guilty of some serious offense, he may stay at his post till death. Thus we sometimes see huge city parishes which would tax even the strongest remain in the hands of octogenarians. Why, not a single grocery store could survive with such an old manager as these parishes have!

A religious, on the contrary, is not irremovable. Rather, he is at the disposition of his superiors, secular and religious, and not only does Canon Law not grant him any rights but his whole religious ideal keeps him from even desiring any. Free from ridiculous dreams of advancement, he knows he need not make a career for himself. Consequently, when age makes him inefficient, there is nothing to keep his superiors from giving him a less responsible position or sending him to a smaller parish. Many of us who were pastors are now curates once again—and without any bitterness. It is reassuring for a young man to know that as soon as he overrates himself and his responsibilities, as soon as self-love threatens to outstrip his zeal, his superior will step in and keep him from becoming useless or prejudicial to the cause.

Never for a moment would we think of drawing a parallel between the life of a secular priest and that of a religious. Never would we extol the religious life at the expense of the other, attributing a special virtue to it or calling it a safe harbor while criticizing the life of a secular priest as being full of danger. We are not boasting or patting ourselves on the back. All we are saying is this: we have realized both our own weakness and the problems and perils that beset us, and, unwilling to live our entire priestly life amid the fluctuations of an unending war, we have chosen the religious life as a protection, as a staff to support us, and especially as a means of maintaining in our hearts the fervor of our youth.

We must finish our inventory, however, before exposing at length the essence and the glory of the religious ideal.

Let us consider the many ways in which a congregation helps its members live their priesthood to the full. First of all, there is the novitiate—a difficult period of testing, a serious preparation for the priesthood. It is a time of chiseling and polishing which finally fashions the workingman's priest.

Far from being purely negative and austere, the novitiate is a group of young men, strangers till yesterday, who know at first sight that they have all shared the same dream and want to dedicate their whole life to it. They are in the novitiate, not only to study as in the seminary, but to develop their character and strengthen their will together. For an entire year they work hand in hand, with the tools of prayer, penance and meditation, to become more and more like their ideal. Emulation for them looks beyond scholastic or technical achievement to moral perfection and union with God. Together they try to increase their love for the poor and the working class and to equip themselves for the mission awaiting them.

Almost beyond imagining are the benefits to be derived from a year of spirituality (either before or after the regular seminary studies) which they discuss among themselves, think out anew, and above all apply to their daily lives. At every step of their ministry, in years to come, that particular training will assist them both in giving spiritual direction and in preaching retreats and days of recollection. That year will be fruitful from even a purely practical viewpoint.

The novitiate reaches its consummation in the vows,

which stand like guards strategically posted at the three most vulnerable approaches to the human heart. Indeed, the temptations to amass riches, yield to the flesh, and become proud and independent assail a priest his whole life through; and though the vows, we repeat, do not confirm a religious in virtue, they do serve as three points on which superior and subject may focus their attention and concentrate their efforts.

After our Lord Jesus Christ had fasted forty days in the desert, the devil tempted Him. The temptations Christ underwent before entering upon His ministry have been recorded in the gospel, not by chance, but because they illustrate so well the three chief temptations that beset the apostle, and, specifically, the apostle of today. It seems as though Christ, full of justice and virtue, thought immediately of those who would continue His mission, and willed to warn them at the very beginning of the gospel against the major pitfalls that lie in their path.

"Since thou art hungry, bid these stones become loaves of bread." Just as Satan tempted Christ to use His power in order to satisfy His hunger, so may an apostle, and particularly a pastor, be tempted to use his ministry as a means of acquiring, over and above the necessities of life, things that will afford him comfort and ease.

"Cast thyself down from the temple and, if thou art the son of God, angels will come to hold thee up." Again, just as Satan tempted Christ to do something spectacular in order to win over the rabble, so may a priest be subtly tempted to leave the beaten path and strike out on his own, to be different and even seek a bit of adventure, to concentrate on the unusual and the striking on the pretext of spreading the kingdom of God.

"I will give thee all the kingdoms of the world if only thou wilt fall down and worship me." Satan thought he could dazzle Christ with earthly kingdoms. Christ, of course, was above that, but many of His disciples are sorely tempted to seek their own little kingdom instead of His. They make the parish their court and gather about themselves a circle of penitents, followers and admirers.

Setting aside the vow of chastity, which holds for secular as well as for religious priests, we see that the other vows, poverty and obedience, are ever-watchful sentinels set about the apostle's heart to rout temptation.

Furthermore, since resolutions and promises and even vows are not proof against time, religious have their rule to help them remain faithful till death. Naturally, there is a world of difference between a sincere quest for the spirit of the rule and a slavish adherence to the letter of it. The ideal, in any religious institute, does not consist in duplicating the founder's achievements literally; it consists in finding out and doing whole-heartedly what he would do if he were living today. Still, we should not look down our noses at strict obedience and conscientious observance of details. The rule is always there to urge religious on when fervor has cooled and when, alone, they would not see clearly or have the courage to go further.

Among the many provisions of the rule, some—monthly and yearly retreats, for example—are especially useful and enable a religious to get his bearings periodically. In a religious congregation such retreats are not optional and nothing about them is left to the choice and good will of the retreatants. The silence, the reaffirming of ideals by the superior, the whole atmosphere of the retreat house—all these are carefully calculated to make a religious face essential facts and to cast a new light on things which may have grown dim in his mind during his year's ministry.

Even more deep-rooted and all-pervading than the rule is the common ideal that unites the members of any congregation. Obviously, they did not all join it with the same identical outlook, and they invest that ideal with a variety of tints and hues. Though time may even alter particular points of view, yet it is quite true that in every congregation there is a spirit which takes shape and lives on. If born of self-sufficiency and pride, that spirit may well prove a paralyzing agent; but if it is to animate the apostles our modern world needs, it must be conceived and constituted by young souls, strong, noble and daring.

On certain days, when our work is difficult and we keep reaping disappointment, discouragement dogs our steps. If at such times we see a team at work around us and remember that the older men have known the same trials and that the younger ones are looking ahead to them confidently, plunging into the fray with enthusiasm, we will very likely be able to fight off discouragement. Alone, a man may be a prey to discouragement; surrounded by his brethren, he can conquer it.

Chronologically, the last advantage a congregation offers is a home where old or sick priests may retire. Some may smile to hear us call it an advantage, a prop, an encouragement; and the young will surely say, "We'll see about that."

Certain professions offer their members the prospect of such a home as a haven of rest. That is not what we are doing; we do not invite young men to join our Institute so they may sit back and relax some day. But we do say this: it is difficult to imagine what a blessing such a house can be throughout life.

As we stated earlier, a religious need not worry about the future or provide for his old age. If he works and spends himself without reserve, God, through his superior, will take care of the future. This certainty makes it easier for a priest to submit his resignation when he knows the time has come.

Some may look scornfully at these old priests and make irreverent remarks that approach blasphemy. Yet what a warm, comforting atmosphere surrounds a gathering of tired apostles who have labored at different phases of the same work! How many old warriors in these houses look with joy at what the young are doing, applaud their undertakings, and fall asleep happy in the peace of the Lord because they know the work will go on!

May our Institute provide ever greater power and dynamism for the coming generations so that more generous, enlightened and loving apostles may rise up among the poor and the working class. Our Institute is only a means, but may it be the efficacious means of promoting the kingdom of God among all the outcasts.

PART TWO

SHEPHERDS MAKE TRUER

RELIGIOUS

by

ABBÉ R. MEURICE

CHAPTER I

THE OTHER SIDE OF THE PICTURE

Let us be realistic. Though the many advantages of religious community life do a great deal to make pastoral work more effective, should we consider that life a "crutch," as do the seminary rectors who recommend it to undecided, wavering subjects? Most certainly not. Writing about the Carmelites, Bernanos said something which holds true for every form of the religious life. He declared, "It is not the rule which upholds us, it is we who uphold the rule."

Teamwork among priests does not produce unfailing results. It presupposes good will and wholehearted devotion on the part of each member, and, in addition, a community of prayer and a brotherly approach to God and souls.

Here is a young priest who wants to devote himself entirely to the apostolate. Does he not have reason to fear that in the pastoral ministry greater scope would entail a loss of intensity and completeness? He wonders whether the many and ceaseless activities of a parish priest will hinder his interior activity, his prayer, and that divine life which was just beginning to blossom when he left the seminary.

Here is another. His whole life is the glory of God, the beauty of His house, the splendor of His worship; and he wants to communicate that love to others. Will he be able to in parish life? Afraid of that paradoxical vocation, many have thought not and have refused to take a chance. And their objections are not unfounded, for "activism"—that is, activity divorced from spirituality—is the most common form of those temptations that hound the parish priest.

To anyone who wants to use them the religious life offers the spiritual resources mentioned above. We have already said that parish life can be a school of asceticism and a constant invitation to humility, self-denial and mortification; and it seems that we could discern in the interior life of true shepherds of parishes, such as Père Anizan, all the nights described by the masters of the spiritual life.

Would it be too much to say that parishes can also be schools of the interior life, of prayer and even mysticism? Can they do for the religious-priests that serve them what convents and monasteries do for the others? Is it possible for a religious, as shepherd of a parish, to keep his spiritual life unimpaired in spite of his parish or thanks to extra-parochial aids? And, even more to the point, is it possible for him to develop that spiritual life in and through the exercise of his parish ministry? We think it is, and we honestly believe we are right.

After the priest has anointed a newly baptized baby's head with chrism, he turns from prayer and exorcism, speaks to the infant Christian and gives it two commands. Placing a white linen cloth on the child's head, he says, "See thou carry it unstained before the judgment seat of our Lord Jesus Christ"; and giving it a lighted candle, he urges, "See thou guard the grace of thy baptism without blame; keep the commandments of God, so that when the Lord shall come to call thee to the nuptials, thou mayest meet Him with all the saints." As is evident from these words and actions, the Church knows full well that all is not done when the sacrament has produced its immediate and unfailing effect —*ex opere operato,* as the theologians say. Rather, with the free co-operation of the Church and her newly baptized subject, grace tends to attain to the fulness of reality. So it is with all the sacraments. Christ offers us life; and if we want it, we have to reach for it spontaneously, keep striving for it, and always strengthen our desire for it. As Jesus said to the rich young man, "If thou wilt . . ."

Grace is granted, the interior self is established, the new man is born. But he has to grow; or, as the moderns would doubtless have it, he must become "existential." Now, that is the work of each individual soul. With the help of grace and his own efforts, everyone must become actually what baptism, confirmation and holy orders have already made him potentially. Between the being which is given to us and full development we must ever strive, because there exists here a tension, and from that tension springs the tendency toward the perfection of charity which is essential to the religious life.

Just as Christ, desiring to reach all the faithful, has given the Church the mission of bringing them the sacraments (and her way of doing so varies according to time and place), so also do the faithful, desiring to answer the divine call, give the Church the mission of offering their will to God. To this end, she uses a means which was formerly called the apostolic life. Now known as the religious life, it is growing in depth and breadth according to the needs of each generation.

By the act of religious profession, Holy Mother Church raises her children's faith to the dignity of "the sacrifice and service of the faith" which Saint Paul mentions to the Philippians.[1] By that same act of religious consecration she effectually fulfills the death to the world and the resurrection in Christ the Conqueror which were wrought ritually at baptism.

No doubt, we can become saints some other way and sink into mediocrity even as religious; nevertheless, it is true that the religious life has the *a priori* approval of the Church. Of this the Holy Father reminded us explicitly at the recent congress of religious held in Rome. He declared: "It has been decreed by divine law that clerics form a class apart from laymen. Between these two groups of the hierarchy there lies the religious life, which, having originated within the Church, derives its

[1] Philippians 2:17

raison d'être and its worth from the fact that it is so
closely bound up with the purpose of the Church—
namely, the sanctification of mankind. If every Christian
is bound to set that sacred goal before himself under
the guidance of the Church, religious strive toward it
by a special path and by more elevated mea..s." [2] Now,
in sanctioning this mode of life, the Church is not only
looking out for the good of individuals. Since its own
perfection and that of any Catholic are two aspects of
one and the same reality, she is actually looking out for
her own good. That is why religious profession is the
Church's concern as much as the individual's. It is
effected by the Church, for the Church and in the
Church.

I. BY THE CHURCH

This is the canonical aspect of the question. A glance
at the Code or at the history of religious foundations is
enough to show with what care and precaution the
Church surrounds the founding, the development and
the safe-keeping of her religious orders and institutes
even on the diocesan level. There can be no such thing
as a real religious institute without her permission and
approval. Those who played a part in the founding of
the Sons of Charity remember how scrupulously Père

[2] See *Documentation catholique,* December 31, 1950, column
1670.

Anizan heeded the directives of Rome and how he rejoiced at the unusual and unexpected ways in which he received the various decrees that led his infant congregation to definitive approbation.

II. FOR THE CHURCH

These canonical requirements are justified by the theological aspects of the question. The Church on earth is the habitual manifestation of God's glory to men. She is that especially because of the qualities we call "marks" —oneness, holiness, catholicity and apostolicity—all of which have to be regularly visible in order to be marks at all. Now, that is precisely the role of religious societies: to manifest the glory of God our Lord to men by bearing witness to the marks of the Church, and particularly her holiness. Thus we understand why a certain amount of notoriety (or general knowledge, if you prefer) has to surround religious profession. Unlike vows springing from devotion, which are personal and private matters, profession is something public and social. The garb of the religious attests to it, as do his name and his title. From this point of view it would seem contradictory to be a religious incognito, since the Church cannot hide her holiness but must let it shine out for all to see. Her religious families are schools of holiness where everyone may learn.

Could there be a nobler motive for entering the religious life than the desire to show forth the Church's holiness to the best of one's power in an approved order? Let us underline the fact that this is a matter of common holiness; and by common holiness we mean, first, the achievement of a body rather than of individuals, and, secondly, an ordinary level of virtue which will in some cases become heroic.

III. IN THE CHURCH

The words "in the Church" are to be taken, not in a quantitative, but rather in a substantial sense. The religious life is not an added jewel which the Church may wear; it is the Church herself in her Mary-like calling as spouse and servant of the Lord. The concept of Church-without-religious seems incomplete because religious profession is but the logical development of that first profession and promise made at baptism. When her children are baptized, when she clothes them in the garments of God's servants, when she helps them hear the call of the Spouse, then the Church is sharing with each and every Christian her own calling as spouse of Christ. And the religious call merely confirms that first call.

The religious vocation is really one of the Church's vocations; and that holds true of monks and cloistered nuns as it does of the religious, male and female, in all the orders and institutes approved by the Church.

We are now in a position to appreciate the ancient formula used by the Premonstratensians when taking their vows: "I offer my very self to the Catholic Church." We have had to cover all this ground so that we might now show how these principles will affect a religious who is serving in a parish as its pastor.

CHAPTER II

THE PARISH AS A SOURCE
OF HOLINESS

The mien of the Church varies with her different religious orders and institutes. Hierarchic and family-like
in the monastic orders, she appears as a teacher of truth
in the teaching congregations. Missionaries prove her
catholicity, hospitalers her motherly love, and so on with
all the different callings. For our purposes, let us consider the religious who is also a shepherd of souls. He
has contemplated the Church from a special viewpoint
which becomes concrete in the parish.

Poring over maps of Paris and marking out the over-
populated sections, Père Anizan tried to determine
where he might most effectively establish the various
houses needed to carry on his work. Like a mother, his
every prayer was heavy with the soul of the city which
he would someday entrust to his followers. So did the
Curé d'Ars, arriving in his new parish, fall upon his
knees when he first saw its belfry and rooftops. From a
distance he saw the panorama of houses and smoking
chimneys, the surrounding fields and the peasants at

work in them. He saw the steeple of the church where he would say Mass, hear confessions and preach. But, beyond seeing, his soul reached out and touched the soul of that parish. That is why he fell on his knees. The two souls communicated together. The parish became his parish and from that moment he carried it in his heart.

In our mind, the concept of "parish" is threefold. Without wishing to seem pedantic, we should like to analyze it with the help of a few terms used in sacramental theology.[1] According to the theologians we may distinguish three features in the notion of "sacrament." They are: 1) the sensible sign, *sacramentum tantum*—as, for instance, bread and wine in the Eucharist; 2) the *sacramentum et res,* which results unfailingly from the sign—the body of Christ present under the sacred species, for example; and 3) the *res tantum,* or the profound reality to which the sacrament leads—in the Eucharist, the unity of the Church.

We may apply these ideas to the parish.

1. The visible sign of a parish is its *human aspect*— a determinate group of people with their technical, economic and social characteristics, located in a specific place, and subject to certain influences. These facts will

[1] As we use them, these terms are analogical. Following St. Thomas, theologians have given them a precise, technical meaning which cannot apply here. Nevertheless, we believe that the affinity between the idea of the Church (and consequently of the parish) and the idea of a sacrament not only justifies a comparison between them but even establishes a solid analogy.

be the object of a sociological investigation which should take into account the history of the group as well as its possibilities for the future. This human aspect corresponds to *sacramentum tantum.*

2.   In the group just discussed there are a certain number of Christians. They constitute the Church in their locality. We can call them the *Catholic aspect* of the parish, the *sacramentum et res,* the meeting place of the material and the spiritual elements of the sacrament. The same faith, hope and charity will join all these baptized persons—Easter Catholics, practicing Catholics and militant Catholics—into one community or family at the altar rail. And that community must bear witness to the gospel in the world, especially in its own neighborhood and within the bounds of the parish, without prejudice to the other social factors which link the various parishes to the diocese and the Church, the county and the nation.

3.   The deepest part of this concept of the parish is the wondrously exalted goal toward which God has ordained that parish in and through the Catholic Church. Just as every man can be called a world in miniature, a microcosm, so each parish is the universal Church in miniature. That is the *mystical,* the truest, aspect of the parish (*res tantum*). Ontologically speaking, it is the prime aspect; and though a priest with the insight of faith will discover it in a flash, centuries of effort will be required to realize it and bring it to light. For it is the everlasting Church we are talking

about, the holy and spotless spouse Saint Paul describes, the new Jerusalem of the Apocalypse already being built up in souls and in the community of souls, which, as we have said, are two parts of one great reality.

Corresponding to each level, each value, in the concept labeled "parish," there are three aspects to the vocation of a shepherd of souls. They are three phases of the same truth; and, without wishing to separate them artificially or set them up in opposition to one another, we can say this: 1) corresponding to the "mystical" value there is the priest's primordial function, which we shall call "typological" or exemplary; 2) corresponding to the "Catholic" value of the parish there is his "liturgical" function; and 3) corresponding to the "human" value, his "missionary" function. And we want to add that the religious-pastor will find his threefold function eminently sanctifying.

I. THE PRIEST'S TYPOLOGICAL FUNCTION

A parish is not an agglomeration of souls. We have just said that the holiness of individual Catholics coincides with the holiness of the Church. To the Corinthians (hardly a community of cloistered nuns, it seems) Saint Paul wrote the following words, now used as the Epistle in the common of virgins: "Would to God that you coud bear with a little of my foolishness! Nay, do bear

with me, for I am jealous for you with a divine jealousy.
For I betrothed you to one spouse, that I might present
you a chaste virgin to Christ." [2] Notice that he changes
from the plural in "I have betrothed you" to the singular
in "a chaste virgin." What he is offering to Christ is the
entire Corinthian Church, yet his offering would be
meaningless unless each and every soul heeded his
words. Thus souls appear to be concentric. And the
shepherd is no exception; far from being something
apart from his flock, his soul must not only be fused
with that flock but must even distend so as to carry it.
Is that not what Saint Peter meant when he urged
shepherds of souls to become "a *pattern* to the flock"? [3]
Saint Paul used the same word in the same sense on
several occasions, as, for instance, when he wrote to
the Philippians: "Be imitators of me, and mark those
who walk after the *pattern* you have in us." [4]

Saint Peter reminds his presbyters that their prime
duty is, not to lord it over their charges, but to become
"from the heart a pattern to the flock." For want of a
more common term which would also be satisfactory,
we have described the first function of a religious-pastor
as "typological"—an adjective coined from the Greek
tupos, which is rendered in Latin as *forma* and in Eng-
lish as "pattern." Exegetes tell us that *tupos* has a very

[2] II Corinthians 11:1-2
[3] I Peter 5:3
[4] Philippians 3:17

special meaning in the New Testament and has to be considered in relation to a complimentary term, *antitupos*, which Saint Peter uses elsewhere in the same Epistle.[5] Discussing baptism, he says it is the "counterpart," the *antitupos*, of Noe's ark, which is the *tupos*. The ark is a shadow, an outline or an image of another reality which will exist in the state of perfection— namely, the sacrament of baptism.

The shepherd of souls, then, is to become the living pattern of his flock. But where will he find his own model and goal if not in the spouse of Christ, the Church, that definitive, eternal and perfect reality toward which his whole parish strains?

We are now at the very heart of the matter. Because of his role as shepherd, the religious-priest must in his own soul try to realize that spousal calling with relation to the eternal pattern of his flock. That is his duty as a shepherd. On profession day, moreover, he ratified ritually, canonically and officially the vocation which baptism had given him as an individual—a vocation like the Church's: to be the servant and the spouse of Christ. So we see how his duty as a shepherd will help him mightily to live his profession as a religious, since both duty and vow fuse his whole existence with the same mystery.

Thus we see how such a conception of his calling can quicken the spiritual life of a religious. His prayer can

[5] I Peter 3:21

be one long contemplation of the mystical reality which belongs both to him and to his flock. Faith and prayer will simplify his outlook until he always sees the same profound reality in each of his parishioners, in each group, in his congregation every Sunday and in the entire area committed to him.

By reason of his calling a religious is bound to a community. In parish life that is a great advantage, for the shepherd-team discussed in Part One of this book can serve in its own way as "a pattern to the flock." The community-team in the rectory is the nucleus around which the faithful will gather, drawn and held there by love and obedience to pray together, to praise God and help the neighbor.

This mystical view of his vocation contains the theological basis for the devotion every religious-pastor should have toward our Lady. Being the fulness of the Church, she is really the pattern of his parish, and he will make her that by praying and consecrating his flock to her. This is where we see the reason behind Saint Grignion de Monfort's consecration to Mary as her slave. A striking example of its efficacy is the story of Abbé Desgenettes, who, having consecrated his flock to the Immaculate Heart of Mary, could no longer keep count of the victories she won over his parish and beyond.

Far from drawing a religious away from his ideal and first fervor, then, pastoral work makes him understand that ideal more deeply and realize it a little better with every passing day.

II. THE PRIEST'S LITURGICAL FUNCTION

A small community of the faithful (*sacramentum et res*) witnesses to the gospel in the midst of a world which is still pagan. That community is the regular channel chosen by God to dispense His word and His mysteries in their fulness.

Before going on, however, we should like to ask the theologians this question: We understand very well that the sacraments are designed for the good of man, and we give them as well as we can to those persons whom the manuals call "our subjects." But do not we ourselves derive any benefit from administering the sacraments? Can we always be handing out grace without any of it sticking to us? As Saint Paul said, "The farmer who toils must be the first to partake of the fruits." [6]

All we remember from our seminary studies on the subject is that a priest who administers the sacraments in the state of mortal sin commits a sacrilege every time he does so. But what about the priest who administers them in the state of grace? To put it mathematically, we can state the problem this way: the state of mortal sin is to sacrilege as the state of grace is to X. And

[6] II Timothy 2:6

indeed it is an unknown quantity we are looking for—unknown, but certainly not equal to zero.

When we contrast the state of grace with the state of mortal *dis*grace, we are dealing with a dynamic entity. In proportion as a priest wilfully clings to his sin, each sacramental act does him greater harm (except in cases of extreme need) and his sacrilege becomes more formal. On the other hand, the more a priest grows in grace (and we have seen the effect of religious profession on the original grace of baptism), the more will sacrilege's opposite—the X in our equation, the mysterious unknown we should so like to investigate—grow and increase. Thus one and the same thing is to some "an odor that leads to death" and to others "an odor that leads to life . . ." Please Heaven we may be "the fragrance of Christ for God." [7]

If our reasoning is correct, and we honestly believe it is, the religious-priest serving in a parish is in an enviable position: everything that Christ gives him to accomplish his mission he can use to effect the mystical relation which he contemplates in the depths of his soul. Just as Abraham sent his faithful servant to find a wife for Isaac, and the servant, Eliezer, "set out with a variety of his master's treasures," so the parish priest, deputized to present his own parish to Christ as a spouse "in all her glory, not having spot or wrinkle or any such thing, but . . . holy and without blemish," [8] sets out on the

[7] II Corinthians 2:15-16
[8] Genesis 24:10; Ephesians 5:27

night of his ordination with his hands full of the divine riches we call sacraments and sacramentals.

Like Eliezer, he first meets her near a fountain—that fountain which it is his special privilege to unseal on Holy Saturday, that sacred fountain which is as fully given into his care as the tabernacle. That is where the Church receives the cleansing and sanctifying "nuptial bath" Saint Paul alludes to.[9] That first bath is administered again and again in the life of every Catholic by means of the sacrament of penance. The pastor even has universal power over his parishioners, and it is he who will lead them to the threshold of the last Meeting as he repeats, in extreme unction, the gestures, anointings and rites of baptism. With this in mind we feel compelled to quote, as an example of the interior life quickened by the liturgy, the following exhortation from the ritual used in German dioceses. No priest can help making acts of faith, hope and charity as he reads it to a parishioner who is about to appear before God. As at baptism, the priest places a lighted candle in the believer's hand and says:

Dearly beloved brother,
Jesus Christ is the light of the world;
It is He whom you see when you look at this light.
Feast your eyes upon it,
Rejoice because you are not falling asleep in eternal death.
Christian soul, depart;

[9] See Ephesians 5:26

Tear yourself away from this passing life
And go forth to meet your well-beloved Spouse, Jesus Christ,
With this glowing light in your hand.
And may He who has called you to go out of the darkness
Into His radiant light
Not allow you to sink into the kingdom of night;
But rather may He lead you from the shadow of death
Into everlasting light.
May the light of our holy Faith
And the fire of eternal love
Never be extinguished in your mind and your heart.
And do you, holy angel of light,
Protect our brother from all the spirits which rise from the pit
    of endless night,
So that, thanks to your might and your wise workings in his
    heart,
Both hope and love may ever shine.
Amen.

This wonderful reading moves us because it is new to us, and that is why we chose it. Still, it is the same voice we hear in every phrase of the liturgy, in the formulas and prayers used for sacraments and sacramentals. To be fully alive, we must, first, live on that mystical reality which holds true for the faithful as well as for the priest, and, secondly, allow our whole being to be flooded with the grace of the sacrament deposited there by the bishop. The sevenfold sacramental Christ dwells in us priests from the day of our consecration by the bishop.

The ministry places a priest-religious in the full

stream of the life that flows from the glorified Christ. The sacrament of orders seems to afford him the most favorable surroundings. But, as its name indicates, that sacrament is essentially organic; it not only creates priests but it forms the priestly body through which Christ the Priest works in the Church. The hierarchy of its functions proves our statement. In the mystical, or ecclesiastical, body of Christ, the priesthood—or, rather, the assembly of priests—resembles what biologists call a "system," as, for example, in the expression "nervous system." Like any living person, the priestly system has its own life, laws, circulation, and reciprocity of causes and effects.

The moment his superiors assign him to a parish, a religious accepts its condition as his own. He becomes a member of the diocesan family of priests, and they become his brothers. On the parochial level—with the members of the same community-team and with his fellow priests in the deanery or the archdeaconry, whether praising God in the Divine Office or preaching the word of God in any form or dispensing His holy mysteries—everything calls into play the grace that is in him, the theological virtues and the gifts of the Holy Ghost.

He and his fellow workers will have different temperaments, different qualifications and backgrounds—so different, in fact, that, if theirs were a human enterprise, it would be doomed to failure. Through these many facets, however, there shines one same mystery, since there is only one Priest, the one who gives unity to the team of priests and without whom it would immediately disintegrate. The religious-priest knows well that he should not count on human virtue in a parish, on interest, or even on devotion to a common task to sustain a team of priests. He knows that the only thing he can count on is the grace of Christ the Priest, whom he tries to see and venerate in his brethren who share the same priesthood though they are so different from him.

The parish priest is even more dependent upon the bishop of the diocese than upon his fellow priests. Through the bishop he is in direct contact with the source of the sacrament of orders and consequently with the whole sacramental order. We can say of bishops what Père Dunwell said of the apostles: "They are the open door through which the mystery of the Redemption shines out over the world. They are the channel through which the risen Christ draws men closer to the sources of salvation—namely, Christ Himself and death and resurrection in Him." [10]

More than any other mission, parish ministry allows a religious to work together with his bishop. He does not just spend a few hours being ordained by a practically anonymous bishop. He is not dependent in a purely jurisdictional way, like a visiting confessor or retreat master. His relationship is not restricted to a ritual reference in the Canon of the Mass to a bishop he scarcely knows. No, the religious-shepherd belongs to his bishop, and we may even say his superiors have

[10] *La Résurrection de Jésus*, p. 331.

given him to the bishop. He must see things as the bishop does and act in accordance with his wishes. He must look upon his bishop as the representative of the heavenly Father and of Christ in His triple role as King, Priest and Prophet. And he must find in his bishop the source of the perfection which he, by his religious profession, is bound to strive for and which the bishop, by his episcopal consecration, exemplifies and communicates.

For all the holiness placed in the bishop comes *a parte Christi* and is given him for the Church. Not something to be acquired or practiced, it is a treasure of perfection to be handed on; it is the source of the sacraments. Furthermore, that perfection is greater than any other: it is the perfection of Christ Himself. The bishop wears his mystical wedding band and shows forth the chastity of Christ as Spouse of the Church. If before his consecration as a bishop he belonged to a religious institute, he still remains closely associated with that institute in order to assure his personal progress in the spiritual life; but at the same time he is dispensed from the vow of obedience since, being Christ, he owes obedience to the Father alone.

By reason of his ordination and the powers granted him, a priest is very intimately united to Christ in the person of the bishop. Even as a subdeacon, he shares in the celibacy which manifests to the Church the fidelity of her divine Spouse. As a religious besides, he tries to attain to the perfection held out to him at baptism. That perfection is something he must constantly work at and it lets him share the poverty, chastity and obedience of the Church, the servant and spouse of Christ. It is something which he will desire all the more vehemently because, as a shepherd, he knows it is the "pattern for his flock." Thus the religious-pastor stands on a mystic peak where Christ and the Church meet.

This mysterious meeting is fully realized on earth in the Eucharist, which he celebrates in the parish church. It will often lack the splendor and solemnity found in monasteries, but how meaningful will be the words *"nos servi tui sed et plebs tua sancta,"* for the religious-priests are there and their holy flock gathers around them in the parish church on Sunday. The clergy calls the faithful together, forms them into a body and breathes life into them. In any convent or monastery the faithful must necessarily be but guests; sometimes they are invited and sometimes only tolerated, but they are always there as spectators at perfect but often enigmatic liturgical ceremonies. But in their parish church they are at home with their priests. They can sing and pray there —in their own way, of course, but to the best of their ability. They share in the sacrifice of the altar by receiving Communion. And even when a priest says Mass in an empty church during the week, his parishioners are there since he carries them in his heart, and they are very close to him while he prays and receives the body of Christ in their name. Truly, Christ and His spouse meet in the priest.

Some will object: "You don't have to be a religious to do that." Of course not. The Curé d'Ars was a saintly pastor and yet he was not a religious in the canonical meaning of the word. We cannot deny the fact, but from the opposite viewpoint we would add this: a religious has to serve in a parish in order to enjoy all these advantages.

III. THE PRIEST'S MISSIONARY FUNCTION

One of the laws of the Church's sacramental life is the unfailing motion of grace which, released by the sign and the words that accompany it, passes from the thing signified to the profound and mysterious reality toward which the sevenfold organism of the sacraments is wholly oriented. The three steps are constant, necessary and follow an unchanging order.

This holds good for the life of the parish, which is a cell of the entire Church. Let us examine the process now, starting at the end and going back to the beginning. We shall say that the pastor, having glimpsed that unfathomable and mysterious reality with the help of faith and the Holy Spirit, has concretized it by means of the sacraments in his own flock. He now has to propose that reality to everyone else who lives within the boundaries of his parish. In doing so, he will have to respect the workings of grace, just as with the sacraments. Normally, the gospel will be brought to the masses by the faithful rather than through the direct intervention of the priest. In some exceptional cases, of course, the priest has to take the place of the layman, just as it sometimes happens that a layman—and even an unbeliever—has to do duty for a priest. God always needs men. But parishes are not founded on an exception to the general rule, and they could not exist without such a core of the faithful.

Now, there is one sacramental reality—exceptionally rich in mystical significance—which is the exclusive lot of the faithful since it is reserved to them by Church law. We mean marriage. From the beginning of time and right through sin and the flood [11] marriage has been held out to mankind as a sign of God's love. Scripture, particularly from Osee on, consistently supports this view.[12] By making it a sacrament Jesus gives that sign the extraordinary power of being efficacious. Thus, no matter how de-Christianized our parishes are, Catholic homes stand as beacons for everyone to see; they awaken people and make them look for an explanation; they show forth the love of God and, what is more, they produce what they stand for. Here again Saint Paul has something to teach us when he tells the Ephesians: "This [marriage] is a great mystery—I mean in reference to Christ and to the Church." [13]

Because of the faithful who are sanctified by mar-

[11] See the second special prayer at the Nuptial Mass.
[12] See Osee, Chapter 2.
[13] Ephesians 5:32

riage, the profound mystical reality of the parish begins to dawn upon the community. Thus they come to know a mystery which would remain hidden if it were not discovered by faith, explored in silent prayer by the priest, handed on to the faithful by means of the sacraments, and then proposed to those who have not the faith by those who do. "In this matter of the apostolate does the sacrament of matrimony go beyond baptism and confirmation? And if so, does it only allow two Catholics to do apostolic work, each on his own and in his own way? No. Because of the sacrament, it is the couple itself, as a unit and as a cell of the Church, which must carry on such work. The doctrinal basis of this truth, which so few understand as yet, is found in a sublime mystery which Saint Paul expounds and which bride and groom are invited to contemplate and imitate as well as they can. That mystery, brought to their attention during the wedding ceremony, is the union of Christ and His Church for the salvation of mankind. We cannot gauge the influence which a Christian family, intimately united in Christ, exercises over a parish and a neighborhood." [14]

In view of this statement we understand why Père Anizan, when mapping out our parish apostolate, set up as our first objective the restoration of the Christian family. Since every major achievement of Catholic Action starts with the family, the family must be the first to be won over, and one of the priest's most urgent tasks

[14] Bishop Guerry, *Lettre pastorale,* February, 1954.

is to deepen the spiritual life of the married couples he meets.

To get back to the religious-pastor, we may ask what he can expect to reap from this field which seems somewhat removed from his immediate domain. It is the parochial clergy who must see to the long-range preparation of the faithful for marriage, the perfect administering of the sacrament, and the keeping of those solemn pledges of unity, indissolubility and chaste fertility which we may call the triple perpetual profession of married lay persons.

What a man and his wife realize symbolically and gradually, a priest realizes definitively, really and immediately. With the sharp insight obtained from constant mental prayer, the reading of Scripture and the liturgy, faith makes the religious-pastor see the profound reality of Christ and the Church as expressed in newly engaged couples, in the bride and groom who stand before him to be married, and in the homes he visits. Faith shows him the reality which dwells there primarily for him, then for the spouses themselves and for everyone with whom they come into contact and to whom they should reveal it.

Unmarried himself, he helps the protagonists in this conjugal mystery to rise above the sensible and the carnal plane which could engulf them. He teaches them the deepest mystical meaning of their life. At times even the faithful will think him a trifle foolish, as Saint

Paul says,[15] but he should remember that that is the lot of any prophet and that the religious life serves as a prophetic, eschatological ferment in the Church. Parachuted from another universe into this one and from the future into the present, he is very conscious of the world's deficiencies, but at the same time he perceives signs of the life to come, "for this world as we see it is passing away." [16]

In an article in *La Vie Spirituelle,* Père Henry, O.P., wrote: "The mystery of man and woman carries me beyond itself into a realm of realities where the Lover is Christ, the Word of God made flesh, and the Beloved is typically Mary, collectively the Church, particularly each of the faithful and especially every consecrated virgin. The union, however, is One, just as the Beloved is One in the Holy Spirit." [17]

No priest can serve as chaplain to a Catholic Action group or as religious counselor to persons engaged in secular pursuits without enriching his own soul thereby. His whole spiritual activity in praying or administering the sacraments acts directly on his state of grace and gives it that "fulness," that *"spiritus pinguedinem,"* which the liturgy refers to in an accommodation of Jeremias' text: *"Inebriabo animam sacerdotum pin-*

---

[15] See II Corinthians 11:1
[16] I Corinthians 7:31
[17] May, 1949, p. 475.

guedine et populus meus satiabitur." [18] To that basic
reality are connected the theological virtues, the virtue
of religion, the moral virtues and the gifts of the Holy
Spirit.

By its very nature, the spiritual activity of a Catholic
Action chaplain calls those virtues and gifts into play.
He has to teach the militant to see things through the
eyes of faith, to judge them supernaturally, and to act
with energy, prudence and wisdom. During retreats and
days of recollection he has to awaken the gifts of piety
and fear of God in souls. And in the course of all these
labors he has to maintain an invincible trust in the incontestable victory of Christ the Conqueror. Now, none
of that is achieved *ex opere operato,* but rather *ex opere
operantis.*

We have just used the words "invincible trust," and
indeed Catholic Action rests on that great theological
virtue. *"Les lendemains qui chantent,"* a brighter to-
morrow—there you have the Promised Land toward
which the entire Church is marching. Unless he
strengthens his own supernatural faith, a chaplain will
be unable to train others—workers or students or anyone—and they will be as quickly beaten down by failure
as they were stirred up by an electrifying congress.
When dealing with a militant worker who is vexed by
all sorts of problems, temporal, moral and spiritual,
what can a priest really offer but a living example of
this divine life? Firmly grounded on motives of faith,

[18] Jeremias 30:14

his trust must be supernatural; and only insofar as it is will he succeed in leading his flock safely between the briars of Marxian presumption, which is a trust without God, and the slough of existentialist despair, which is a lack of trust in everyone and everything.

Bereft of spiritual vigor and resources, a priest would have to use artificial means to keep up his activity. He would display great surface agitation but lack that ground-swell which alone is powerful enough "to root up and to pull down, and to waste and to destroy, and to build and to plant." [19]

[19] Jeremias 1:10

CHAPTER III

OUR THREEFOLD IDEAL

Canonically, the Sons of Charity had been in existence six short years when they held their first general chapter in 1925. At this chapter the Founder read an important paper which he later sent to all his sons in religion with the request that they should make of it the program of their life and apostolate. He called his circular letter "Our Threefold Ideal," using the word "ideal" where today we would use "mysticism" or "spirituality." We might say that in it Père Anizan was summing up the bases of his Institute's whole spiritual life. Listing them as the religious life, pastoral work in parishes, and the apostolate of the poor and the working class, he wrote: "We needed all three, and because we found them here among the Sons of Charity we knew that this is where God wanted us."

Each of these three goals is perfect in itself and has inspired heroes such as Saint Bruno, the consummate model of religious; the Curé d'Ars, the parish priest par excellence; and Abbé Godin, that rare missionary to the workingman. The Sons of Charity do not narrow these goals down to be able to work at all three. Instead, they seek to realize each of them perfectly; and this they do by synthesizing and harmonizing them, understanding and attaining them *per modum unius.*

The preceding chapters have demonstrated the relations between, and the sanctifying power of, the three aspects of parish work which correspond exactly to our triple ideal. To recapitulate, we discussed the mystical aspect, which corresponds to the religious life; the sacramental aspect, which corresponds to the traditional pastoral ministry; and, lastly, the human aspect, which, in a parish consisting mainly of workingmen, presents all the problems raised by the apostolate to the working class.

From a study of Père Anizan's written and spoken teaching and from the fact that he invariably treats of these goals in the same order, we conclude that their mutual relationships are not arbitrary and that we cannot understand or pursue them effectually unless we remember that.

Using the metaphor of a plant, we might say that the root is the religious (or spiritual) life, the stem is pastoral work, and the flower or the fruit is the workingman's apostolate. Using the metaphor of a perfect chord, we might say that the tonic is the religious life, the mediant or harmonizing third is the pastorate, and the dominant (which stands out strongest but derives its resonance and its harmonics from the other two) is the apostolate to the working class. A musician would carry the comparison still further and note the provisional and unsatisfactory character of first and second inversions, which, for our purposes, would mean assigning to the ministry or the apostolate the role of tonic that is reserved exclusively to mental prayer and the spiritual life.

We must, however, observe that the orientation of our Institute toward the working class indicates a reaction of the third end on the two others. Just as a particular flower or fruit determines what type of nourishment the roots will draw from the earth, so will the prayer and the interior life of the Sons of Charity, as well as the orientation they give their parishes, be informed by their very special flower and fruit—work among the poor and the outcasts.

At the end of his circular letter, Père Anizan presents Jesus Christ as the perfect model of the religious, the good shepherd and the evangelizer of the poor. Like any true founder, Père Anizan himself offered the best synthesis of the triple ideal in his own life—and that, from his very first years in the priesthood. After his example, we feel it would take a whole community or the entire Institute to embody the concept of what a Son of Charity should be. And we suffer keenly because we know how short we fall of each of our ideals, because we are aware of how desperately we need help, and because our souls are racked by their attempt to achieve

the oneness of their triple ideal without ever quite suc-
ceeding.

As was said before, the only way to succeed is to
make the most of community life and brotherly teamwork and, above all, to strike ever deeper roots in the
spiritual life. In this connection, it would be useful to
gather Père Anizan's many observations of the subject
and study them in relation to our threefold ideal. We
would then doubtlessly discover the preponderant influence Saint John the Evangelist had on his spiritual life.
The motto "God is Love" comes from John; so do the
Good Shepherd, the Sacred Heart and the basic elements of the theology of the Holy Spirit, the Blessed
Virgin Mary and the sacraments. Saint John is truly the
theologian of love and he seems to have inspired this
saying of Père Anizan's: "We must be love and help
others become love."